P9-BYH-806

THE SECOND INDUSTRIAL REVOLUTION

Business Strategy and Internet Technology

John J. Donovan

**To join a Prentice Hall PTR internet mailing list,
point to: http://www.prenhall.com/register**

**Prentice Hall PTR
Upper Saddle River, New Jersey 07458
http:// www.prenhall.com**

Library of Congress Cataloging-in-Publication Data

Donovan, John J.
    The second industrial revolution: business strategy and internet technology / John J. Donovan
    p. cm.
    Includes bibliographical references and index.
    ISBN 0-13-745621-2
    1. Business enterprises--Computer networks--Management.
  2. Information technology--Management. 3. Reengineering
  (Management)--Case studies. 4. Internet (Computer network)
  I. Title
  HD30.37.D66 1997
  658'.054678--dc21   97-5704
                          CIP

Editorial/production supervision: *Nicholas Radhuber*
Manufacturing manager: *Alexis Heydt*
Acquisitions editor: *Paul Becker*
Marketing manager: *Dan Rush*
Editorial assistant: *Maureen Diana*
Cover design director: *Jerry Votta*

Copyright © 1997 by Cambridge Technology Group, Inc.

Published by Prentice Hall PTR
Prentice-Hall, Inc.
Upper Saddle River, New Jersey 07458

    The publisher offers discounts on this book when ordered in bulk quantities.
For more information, contact:

    Corporate Sales Department
    PTR Prentice Hall
    One Lake Street
    Upper Saddle River, NJ 07458
    Phone: 800-382-3419, Fax: 201-236-7141
    E-mail: corpsales@prenhall.com

Printed in the United States of America
20 19 18 17 16 15 14 13 12

ISBN 0-13-745621-2

Prentice-Hall International (UK) Limited, *London*
Prentice-Hall of Australia Pty. Limited, *Sydney*
Prentice-Hall of Canada, Inc., *Toronto*
Prentice-Hall Hispanoamericana, S. A., *Mexico*
Prentice-Hall of India Private Limited, *New Delhi*
Prentice-Hall of Japan, Inc., *Tokyo*
Prentice-Hall Asia Pte. Ltd., *Singapore*
Editora Prentice-Hall do Brasil, Ltda., *Rio de Janeiro*

Contents

Table of Contents

Dedication

A friend,

Sundar

Products and Companies used in Book

VMS is a registered trademark of Digital Equipment Corp. UNIX is a registered trademark of UNIX System Laboratories. LEGO is a registered trademark of The LEGO Group. Smart Street is a registered trademark of Dun & Bradstreet Corp. StockMaster is a registered trademark of Marketplace.net Inc. Lotus Notes is a registered trademark of Lotus Development Corp. CoolTalk is a registered trademark of Netscape Communications Corp. NetMeeting and dbWeb are registered trademarks of Microsoft Corp. Microsoft Internet Explorer is a registered trademark of Microsoft Corp. Netscape Navigator is a registered trademark of Netscape Communications Corp. Visual Basic 5 is a registered trademark of Microsoft Corp. ActiveWeb is a registered trademark of Active Software. UltraJava and Java are registered trademarks of Sun Microsystems, Inc. Visa is a registered trademark of Visa International. MasterCard is a registered trademark of MasterCard International Incorporated. PeopleSoft is a registered trademark of PeopleSoft Manufacturing. SAP is a registered trademark of SAP AG. Baan is a registered trademark of The Baan Company NV. ActiveX is a registered trademark of Microsoft Corp. PowerBuilder is a registered trademark of Sybase, Inc. Cheerios is a registered trademark of General Mills. Palmtop is a registered trademark of Hewlett Packard Company. VDO Live is a registered trademark of VDOnet, Corp. Surf Watch is a registered trademark of SurfWatch Software. Yahoo! Search Engine is a registered trademark of

Products and Companies used in Book

Yahoo! CU-SeeMe is a registered trademark of White Pine Software, Inc. OpenView and SmartCard are registered trademarks of Hewlett Packard Company. Eagle is a registered trademark of Raptor Systems, Inc. MVS is a registered trademark of IBM Corporation. Cadillac is a registered trademark of General Motors Corporation. Gillette Sensor Excel is a registered trademark of Gillette. MS-DOS, Windows, and Windows NT are registered trademarks of Microsoft Corp. CNN is a registered trademark of Cable News Network, Inc. U.S. News and World Report is a registered trademark of U.S. News and World Report, Inc.

All other products used in this document are trademarks of their respective manufacturers.

About the Author

Professor John J. Donovan has held successful careers in business, academia, government, and technology. Professor Donovan is chairman of Cambridge Technology Group and an adjunct professor at MIT. He has founded several successful companies including Cambridge Technology Partners, and Cambridge Technology Enterprises.

Educated at Yale, MIT, and Tufts, Dr. Donovan was awarded tenure at MIT and taught in Electrical Engineering and Management. He was awarded the Tufts Medical School commendation for outstanding contribution to medicine while an Assistant Clinical Professor of Pediatrics at Tufts University. At Harvard University's JFK School of Government, he lectured in the programs for Strategic Computing. His most recent degree, an honorary Doctorate of Economics, was awarded by Prague University in the Czech Republic. At Yale, he is presently a fellow at Silliman College.

In government, he served on the National Academy Commission on USSR/USA Technology and on the Space Research Advising Committee.

In technology, Professor Donovan's pioneering research and writing formed the basis for compiler design, operating systems, and the three-tiered computing architecture. He has written eight books, including *Systems Programming, Operating Systems*, and, most recently, *Business Re-Engineering with Information*

About the Author

Technology, which have been translated into nine languages. He has five wonderful children.

Acknowledgements

I would like to acknowledge three categories of people that have given the inspiration for and substance of this book.

The first group is my colleagues who contributed to the intellectual framework of *The Second Industrial Revolution: Reinventing Your Business on the Web*, including W.E. Demming, Peter Drucker, Michael Hammer, Michael Porter, Robert Reich, Gary Hammel, and C.K. Prahalad. Their seminal works in the field of business strategy form the basis of this book.

The second group of people is the business executives whose struggles, insights, and personal advice have provided the reality test of the theories presented in the book. They include Chairman Kun-Hee Lee of Samsung Corporation; Lew Platt, president and CEO of Hewlett Packard Corporation; Tommy Thompson, governor of the State of Wisconsin; Robert Palmer, president of Digital Equipment Corporation; Paul O'Neill, chairman & CEO of ALCOA; James Duckworth, head of Information Technology at Unilever; David Allen, chairman of DHL International (UK) Limited; Paul McAvoy, former dean of Yale School of Management; Al Carnesale, chancellor of U.C.L.A.; John Reed, president of Citicorp; Isao Okawa, president & chairman of CSK; Jeremy Coote, president of SAP America; Robert Stephenson, senior vice president of IBM North America; James Unruh, former president of Unisys; Paul Baan, president of Baan; and Bill Gates, president of Microsoft Corp. In addition to these, I must thank the

Acknowledgments

thousands of executives I see each year at Cambridge Technology Group seminars. Hearing all of their questions and concerns has allowed me to see the patterns that inspired the framework of this book.

The third group of people that deserves recognition are those individuals who supported me in the research and writing of this book: Michael Meyer, who was in charge of the project; Massimo Chiocca and Anthony Salas, who made contributions to the technical substance; and Sharon McSweeney, Jared Willey, and Christopher Willis, who organized the visual content. I would also like to recognize the rest of the readers and editors of the book, including Alix Ewert, Meredith Brehm, Michael Wei, Aryeh Primus, Walid Negm, Anand Daga, William Lathrop, Rahma Salie, and Lane Beebe.

I thank my wife, Linda, her for her support and acknowledge the contributions that her Harvard doctoral research made to the business models contained within.

Special recognition to my son, colleague, and friend, John J. Donovan, Jr. who co-authored Chapters 7 and 8. As co-author, his name appears on the front cover concealed below mine.

Preface

Fundamentally, *The Second Industrial Revolution: Reinventing Your Business on the Web* gives an implementation strategy for reinventing business with Internet technology. This involves four steps that correspond to the four parts of the book:

- Formulating the correct business strategies for today (Chapter 1 and 2) and reinvention strategies for the future (Chapter 3).

- Implementing the technological infrastructure to support these new strategies. This involves taking advantage of the Internet revolution (Chapter 4), a step-by-step procedure for implementation (Chapter 5), and case studies with emphasis on business benefits (Chapter 6).

- A framework for understanding the technologies and players associated with the Internet (Chapters 7 and 8).

- Managing the change of your organization, your people, and yourself in order to move forward effectively (Chapter 9).

A note on terminology: the terms organization, business, company, and government agency are used interchangeably. The competitive threats that a government agency faces are no less real than those that corporations face. The demands of constituents on a government agency are as severe as the demands of customers on a corporation.

Introduction

On graduation day at Yale University, President Kingman Brewster personally gave me words of inspiration that are a key to success on a personal, corporate, and global level. As I walked across the stage to receive my degree, he said:

"Keep moving, keep moving, keep moving!"

The basic premise of this book is that, if you don't keep moving by reinventing your organization using business strategies that capitalize on the Internet, you have severely, if not fatally, handicapped your enterprise. In these times of rapid economic and technological change, the saying, "Keep moving" is critical.

Senior management might greet the idea of reinventing their business and utilizing the Internet within their enterprise with great skepticism. The Internet, with its global reach and standard architecture, provides a powerful infrastructure that allows companies to succeed with ever-changing business conditions such as the slowing of inflation in South America, the exodus of manufacturing from Germany, the collapse of the Soviet Union, the opening of the South Korean market, and the massive privatization and deregulation occurring around the world.

This book contains examples of the business strategies used by real organizations. Here, I must have an understanding with the reader. If I give an example of a successful organization, this is in no way an endorsement of that organization or a guarantee of its future success. More importantly, if I give an example of an organization that has followed a bad strategy and is unsuccessful, it does not mean that you shouldn't do business with that organization; nor does it mean that it won't be successful in the future. In fact, the failure that I point out could be the impetus for change that produces an even more successful organization. As a founder, chairman, and investor in some 16 companies, I have experienced the agony and disappointment of business mistakes. My sympathies go to my colleagues who will inevitably be in similar circumstances if they are in business for any length of time.

As evidence to support the premise that to keep moving is critical to strategic business planning, consider businesses that were not afraid to innovate; they kept moving and prospered in the last decade:

- Hewlett Packard kept moving into new product areas and will receive 66% of its revenue this year from products that are less than eighteen months old.

- PepsiCo has garnered significant market shares in water, coffee, and snack food sales.

- Ten years ago, Samsung moved into semiconductors and electronics, and is now No. 1 in VCR production in the world.

- ABB, with its award-winning management structure, has created some 1,500 companies.

- Burns, a 100-year-old Australian trading company, moved into hardware stores and, in the past decade, has become a $2 billion yeast and spice company.

  Businesses that have not kept moving have suffered:

- Digital Equipment Corp. faltered when it held onto its old VMS operating system. Digital not only missed out on the UNIX operating system, but called it "snake oil." As a result of ignoring this advance in technology, the company's size dropped from 160,000 employees to its present 50,000.

- Laura Ashley, a wonderful English company, neared bankruptcy when it kept its focus on its beautiful floral print dresses while women wanted conservative business suits for their changing role in the workplace.

- IBM, while defending its mainframe, missed moving to NT, one of today's dominant operating environments. IBM's decision to ignore the impact of open systems and other rapid-growth areas cost it 200,000 employees and $16 billion in losses.

- Polaroid retained its old-style chemical photography making only minor additions to its cameras instead of moving into digital photography, the new wave of photographic imaging. Failure to reinvent this company has resulted in plummeting stock prices.

Introduction

- Bordens' old management structure failed to grow with its acquisition strategy, causing the collapse of this organization.

   Most books on business trends and market strategies give examples of excellent companies. Chances are that, if the book is more than three years old, the example successful companies that haven't moved forward are now foundering. Some that were foundering have felt the pain and reinvented themselves to success.

   Tom Peter's book, *In Search of Excellence*, highlights fifteen so-called excellent companies. The star of the book is People's Express, which will live forever...in our memories. If the excellent companies used as examples in this book do not reinvent themselves to operate in the ever-changing business world and take advantage of business transactions on the Internet, they too will implode.

   This book is written to help the senior executive in four areas:

- To outline the best business strategies for a company to follow if it wants to survive, thrive, and become a dominant player in the future. Chairman Lee of Samsung Corporation recently echoed a common question that chief executives ask, "What's next?"

- To acquaint senior management with the critical edge that moving their business infrastructure to the Internet can provide their companies. Internet-based business strategies and technological solutions are critical to a company's survival—today and in the future.

- To provide a conceptual framework for all of the players and technologies of the Internet.

- To guide organizations and people through the profound changes associated with these new business strategies and technologies.

The business strategies and technologies in this book are not evolutionary; they are revolutionary!

—Professor John J. Donovan

Part 1

Business Reinvention

1

Keep Moving

The purpose of this chapter is to review the business and information technology (IT) evolution of the past that has led to the business and IT revolution of today.

Business Revolution

First, let's take a brief look at the contributions that some of my colleagues have made in the field of business strategy:

- W. E. Demming's concepts and insistence on a business strategy of total quality management (TQM) contributed significantly to the rise of Japan as a economic power in the '50s. Quality remains as the major added value in today's business strategy.

- Peter Drucker has argued for the last three decades that the purpose of a business is to create a customer, survive, and make contributions to the social environment. Customer focus remains the core of today's business strategies.

- For the past two decades, Professor Michael Porter of the Harvard Business School focused on the strategy of raising barriers to entry into your markets, such as brand names and high-volume production. General Motors and AT&T employed this strategy to dominate their markets. Brand names remain important in the consumer products industry.

- For the last decade, Michael Hammer has argued that business process reengineering (BPR) should replace total quality management; rather than, for example, improving your processes by 20%, you should destroy the processes and reengineer them to be 1000% better. Today, fixing your broken processes by replacing them with substantially better ones is a viable strategy.

- In 1991, Robert Reich, the US Secretary of Labor and faculty member at Harvard University advanced the notion that, in a world where technology allows for global distribution of resources, high value, not high volume, would serve as the barrier to entry. Today, high value is essential.

- My book, *Business Process Re-engineering with Information Technology*, stated that business strategies that led to success in the '70s and '80s were static, whereas the successful strategies of the '90s must be dynamic.

- In 1995, Gary Hammel and C.K. Prahalad argued that an organization has to reinvent all aspects of itself to prepare for the future. They maintained that people who cannot see the future will not be there to enjoy it.

Out of all of these seminal works, which is correct? Why the different approaches?

All of these works are correct. Corporations must integrate all of these strategies as one mosaic, one focused laser beam, in order to survive and prosper in the future. It is not that change is new to business. In Demming's time, corporations changed each decade; in Hammel's time, each year; today, they must change every day.

The major difference in the business climate over the past four decades is the rate of change. Today an executive must follow all of these works as well as the strategies contained in this book. These philosophies build on one another:

- Demming's total-quality focus
- Drucker's good management
- Porter's barrier to entry
- Hammer's business process reengineering
- Reich's high value
- Donovan's dynamic strategies
- Hammel's and Prahalad's reinvention

All of these strategies are necessary for businesses to survive today. This book argues that, in order for today's corporations to survive in the future, they must follow a process of continual reinvention and have the means to implement and support this process; that is, they must use the Internet.

Survival

Just a word about survival: Drucker argued that the basic duty of a corporation is to survive. There are three basic ingredients of survival. Corporations must:

- Be able to withstand a hit

- Evolve

- Be opportunistic

- History has shown that every corporation will face death at some point:

- IBM almost failed to make its payroll in the '60s when the release of its MVS operating system was late.

- Boeing bet the company on a new concept—the 747 Jumbo Jet. Few thought that anyone would buy such a large plane.

- Boeing was close to bankruptcy when it sold the first of what turned out to be the most successful airplane ever.

When a company is near death, it takes leadership, focus, and the will to survive. When a corporation gets hit, it needs appropriate executive, customer, employee, legal, and financial infrastructure to survive.

For an organization to evolve and be opportunistic, it needs dynamic, visionary leaders. The question is whether you are opportunistic enough to take your business to the Internet. Will you be like the Digital of ten years ago, calling UNIX snake oil? Will you be like the IBM of five years ago, calling NT nonindustrial strength? Will you dismiss the Internet as an academic endeavor that only college students will use and claim that it is not for real business applications? If the answer to any of these questions is yes, your business is at risk for failure and almost certain death in the future.

Evolution of Information Technology (IT)

Today, IT support is essential to implementing effective business strategies. Implementation of Drucker's customer-focus strategy would be impossible if such information as profitability by product and customer profiles was not available. Hammer's BPR would be impossible unless a business could coordinate an entire supply-chain process and corresponding information flow. Porter's suggestion of creating a barrier to entry by reaching out to customers would necessitate information-transaction systems.

Now, for the first time in history, a low-cost, global IT infrastructure that can facilitate all of these business strategies exists: the Internet. The Internet provides the means for your business to connect to and interact with some 50 million global users (partners and customers) today and, by some estimates, 500 million in five years! The Intranet (using the Internet standards within your companies network) allows for a flexible standard architecture that can easily incorporate business change and Internet technologies within your organization.

The Internet lets your company conduct business anywhere in the world instantly, inexpensively, and reliably, over a network using standards-based software. What do you do with this? How does it fit into your strategy? The business ramifications of these questions are enormous and potentially overwhelming without the information contained in this book.

How can you help your organization avoid the enormous disappointments and pitfalls that have resulted from previous IT failures to support business? James Morgan, president of Shell Oil Company, told me in a disappointed tone that he spends hundreds of millions of dollars on IT and still cannot get a report on profitability by product. A senior executive at Motorola told me that the average life cycle of a new product is about nine months; on average, it takes two years to build the IT systems to support that product; therefore, the product is dead for fifteen months before its warranty and ordering systems are up and running. David Allen, CEO of DHL International, asked me: "I'm behind Federal Express in my use of the Internet. How do I catch up?" Robert Palmer, president of Digital Equipment Corporation, publicly discussed his frustration at the amount of time it is taking to build his ordering system.

Where does IT and the Internet fit in your business? First, the Internet is more than IT: It is changing the entire landscape of business. The business role of IT has evolved over the past 30 years. In the '60s and '70s, IT supported back-office functions; it automated the manual operations of accounting, payroll, and invoicing. IBM, UNIVAC, and Burroughs were pioneers in producing such IT systems. Later IBM, MIT, and others developed sophisticated transaction and time-sharing operating systems that allowed transaction processing. Computers became essential for assisting the basic business processes of corporations.

It is important to note that IT in the '80s supported static business strategies; hence the software, database, and operating systems of IBM such as CICS and others did not need to accommodate a dynamic environment. Rather, they were designed for robust, static operations. James Morgan's difficulty in using IT to determine profitability by products is not necessarily the IT staff's fault. Shell's growth in the number and type of products outpaced the ability of the old static IT systems to change continuously. The '80s were sad years for CIOs; one-third of them lost their jobs each year.

In 1990 came three-tiered, client/server technologies advocated by Cambridge Technology Group (CTG) and others. CTG pioneered the three-tiered architecture where the separation of the presentation, functionality, and data layers allowed IT to adapt to dynamic business strategies. Those CIOs who moved to a three-tiered, client/server architecture were finally able readily to satisfy the information needs of their users. The systems integrators that followed the CTG architecture prospered such as Cambridge Technology Partners, Hewlett Packard, and c-bridge.

Next came objects or reusable-component software that offered the interconnectability and interchangeability of a LEGO set. The concept of assembling applications in the interchangeable way that automobile components are assembled allowed for rapid development of systems to support rapid business changes. In all these software architectures, however, the underlying networks were private and expensive to set up, maintain, and change.

Then suddenly came the Internet with its astounding growth and explosion of functionality and data. Hewlett Packard, IBM, Microsoft, and CTG, all potential suppliers of Internet services, were totally caught off guard. Today, all of these companies are investing substantial resources into the Internet. CTG, which has created companies for more than a decade and had made no entry into the Internet market before 1996, has created four Internet companies just this year!

The Internet Defined

The Internet comprises two elements:

- A communications network
- A set of software standards

The Internet is a communications network that operates over existing media and telephone lines; it is robust, global, and based on a communication standard called TCP/IP. If private communications lines are used, it is called Intranet; if public lines are used, it is called the Internet.

The Internet is also a set of software standards including the basic functions of email, file-transfer protocols; and web services, including browsers, that find and retrieve information. What is so special about this communication method that will change the way that companies do businesses? Unlike any other communication system in existence, the Internet:

- Is used by millions of people

- Houses vast stores of information from academic, government, corporate, and professional sources

- Has a global reach

- Is inexpensive and reliable to use

- Is a three-tiered, client/server architecture that offers an easy way to upgrade, change, and adapt the communication processes that companies use to transact their business

For example, instead of a manufacturer's customers going to a store that is supplied by a distributor, the customers will be able to order directly from the company's factories, from the comfort of their home PC or special Internet device connected to the Internet via telephone lines. What will happen to distributors? How will stores change? How will online banking services expand? All of these basic business functions will evolve into interactive, online services in the future. This book will show how you can survive and take advantage of business opportunities that the Internet offers.

The Second Industrial Revolution

Seldom in your lifetime will you have the opportunity to witness or be a player in the restructuring of the entire business ecosystem with all of its challenges and opportunities. Companies that choose to move their business to the Internet will achieve rapid market dominance from trading, retailing, and banking at a rate that will outpace their competition.

Will your corporation be like the stagecoach company that did not recognize the impact of the discovery of oil or the advent of the railroad? Or will it be a winner like the automobile and plastic companies that grew out of and thrived on new technology?

Winning means getting your business to the future first. The Internet is the future. If you do not see the Internet as your future, your company will have none. If you do not take your business transactions onto the Internet, you will seriously handicap your business' chances for successful competition and future survival. And survival is the basic responsibility that senior management has to its corporation. If a business does move its transactions and communications to the Internet, it will achieve an unlimited global reach to new customers and markets. The Internet will democratize access to your business. It is a revolution. The Internet will entirely change the way business is done. On the way to this change, will your organization be a driver, a passenger, or roadkill?

2

The Business Revolution

This chapter illustrates the strategies that will help your business survive today. Chapter 3 will present the continual reinvention strategies for the future. Simply put, the strategies that worked in the last decade will lead to failure in today's business world. Strategies from the last decade supported static business that existed in a world changing at what we would today call a glacial rate. Today, all new strategies for survival are dynamic. This chapter will discuss these new strategies and show how the Internet supports each.

Table 1 summarizes the strategies followed by corporations in the past, and the corresponding new strategies that should be followed today in order to survive. Each of these strategies will subsequently be explored in more detail.

TABLE 1. *Business Strategies for Today*

Old	New
1. Stick to brand names	Continually add value
2. Stick to present business	Continually edge into new businesses
3. Stick to established markets	Continually enter niche markets
4. Stick to a steady experience course	Continually eat your own lunch

TABLE 1. *Business Strategies for Today, (Continued)*

Old	New
5. Vertically integrate	Continually enter into partnerships
6. Stick to a local focus	Continually go global; think local
7. Total Quality Management Process	Continual business process re-engineering

1. Old Strategy - Stick to Brand Names

Over the last decade, well-established corporations paid much attention to the promotion of their brand name and relied on it as a barrier to entry to their markets. When I was growing up, the expression "it's a Cadillac" was synonymous with excellence. Today, how many of you aspire to own a Cadillac? The brand name did not survive through Cadillac's poor quality production in the '80s. Laura Ashley's brand name has not helped as it has approached bankruptcy. Likewise, its brand name did not save Hayes, the pioneer in modems, as it also fell into bankruptcy. Even the enormously admired name of IBM did not stop the mass shift of its customers in the '80s and '90s to Hewlett Packard for open systems, which offered more added value. IBM's brand name did not prevent the loss of $16 billion and the layoff of 200,000 people.

New Strategy - Continually Add Value

The key today is to continue to add value to your products and services. Compaq offered warranties on its PCs, Microsoft offered more features on its word-processing software, and the Massachusetts Registry of Motor Vehicles now offers easy license renewal over the Internet.

Note that the contrast between the old model of business strategy and the new one may be more complex for some industries. For example, in mature retail industries, brand names are still very important; but, if they do not add value, those products will wither and die like Tang breakfast drink and Tab soda. In all cases, adding value is key.

Internet Opportunity for Adding Value

The Internet business opportunity for adding value is that the Internet can:

- Provide easy access to information about your business

- Allow customers to order your products and services directly

- Provide videoconferencing repair service

- Help your internal operations run more effectively with an Intranet solution

Furthermore, with the Internet, it is now possible to obtain accurate and immediate feedback from your customers. With access to this information, your business will be able to add the most personalized value to the customer.

2. Old Strategy - Stick To Present Business

This is the strategy of producing the same products and services, only making incremental improvements each year. The problem with this strategy is that, if your business is a good one, competitors will move into the market, leaving you with no alternative as your margins deteriorate. Polaroid has continued to stick to instant photography using chemical processing, only incrementally improving its cameras. This strategy has resulted in a continual loss of market share, falling stock prices, and layoffs; whereas its competitor, Kodak, has reinvented itself around new digital photographic technologies and is thriving.

New Strategy - Continually Edge Into New Businesses

The new business strategy is continually to edge into new businesses. PepsiCo has sequentially moved into the water, coffee, and snack food businesses, while still maintaining its core business of soft drinks. Microsoft has moved into enterprise computing, banking, games, and the Internet while maintaining its core business of desktop computing.

Internet Opportunity for Entering New Businesses

The Internet provides the rapid means to enter new businesses and geographic areas with low infrastructure costs. Recently, after I received an award in the Czech Republic, the president of a small glass company, the pride of the Czech Republic, told me of his dream someday to reach the Asian market. This he said, "was only a dream," not to be realized in his lifetime, as he had no distribution or sales infrastructure in Asia. That evening the CTG team built his company a web site that described the Czech company's products and provided an online ordering capability. Within days, the firm was receiving orders from and shipping its products to Asia.

3. Old Strategy - Stick to Established Markets

Corporations that follow the business strategy of entering such large markets as health, defense, and aerospace, often find strong, entrenched players that are huge obstacles to success in these markets.

New Strategy - Continually Enter Niche Markets

The new business strategy is continually to enter niche markets and grow them. Unilever, the English/Dutch consumer-product giant, entered the niche market of selling ice cream in India, a country where the cow is viewed as a religious symbol. There are, however, roughly 900 million people in India. If Unilever is successful at teaching them to like ice cream, this will be a very good business strategy. Hewlett Packard entered a

17

niche called UNIX in 1985 and has subsequently expanded its share of this market to more than $10 billion. Now it must move into NT. Cross Pens entered the gift pens niche and grew this market.

Internet Opportunity for Entering Niche Markets

The Internet allows you to enter a niche and quickly bring new products and services to customers. It also allows you to get immediate feedback from customers in order to modify your products and services quickly within the niche. Amazon entered the niche of selling books on the Internet. It now dominates that space.

4. Old Strategy - Stick to a Steady Experience Course

This is a strategy by which a corporation focuses only on constantly improving its existing products and services, making them better and cheaper. The problem is that your competitors will see where you are headed and leapfrog you on your experience curve. Dun & Bradstreet kept improving its two-tiered Smart Street software, but was mortally wounded by the introduction of the three-tiered, client/server solutions of SAP and Baan. Laura Ashley kept improving its floral print dresses only to be mortally wounded by competition offering smart professional clothing to the woman of the '90s. Why didn't Laura Ashley offer a professional suit and compete with itself?

New Strategy - Continually "Eat Your Own Lunch"

An alternative and better business strategy is to destroy your old experience curves and create new ones. That is, continually "eat your own lunch;" compete with your own products before someone else does. Gillette has followed this strategy with success. Periodically it comes out with a new razor such as the Sensor Excel that competes with and destroys its previous one (along with destroying the competition).

Internet Opportunity for Eating Your Own Lunch

The Internet provides you with quick means to deliver your new products and services to a vast global market.

5. Old Strategy - Vertically Integrate

The old business strategy was to buy and integrate businesses in your food chain, such as a car manufacturer buying dealers or parts manufacturers. This strategy necessitated the ownership of disparate industries, requiring disparate management styles. General Motors followed this strategy within its manufacturing supply chain and, as a result, has had continually higher costs of production relative to Ford and Chrysler.

New Strategy - Continually Enter into Partnerships

The new business strategy is continually to form partnerships. This allows businesses to focus on what they do best and join with others for additional services, and/or complimentary products. The airlines have been very successful in following this strategy. Delta and Swissair, American Airlines and British Air, KLM and Northwest, and others have partnered to gain access to new markets in geographic areas where they have little or no infrastructure and allowed their partners to service the local markets.

Internet Opportunity for Partnerships

The Internet lets corporations communicate rapidly and inexpensively, and connects the basic information support systems of all partners in their extended enterprise. Groupware products such as NetMeeting provide collaboration among ten of CTG's companies and its corporate law firm.

6. Old Strategy - Stick to Local Focus

In the past, corporations would focus only on a local area; or, at most, the host country. In South Korea, for example, the business model of corporations was to focus on their protected home market. In recent years, saturated internal markets have spurred South Korea's corporations to go global. How does this small "island" expand to every corner of the globe? The Internet is an answer.

New Strategy - Continually Go Global, Think Local

The new business strategy is continually to go global and think local. That is, customize products and services to meet the needs of customers all over the globe.

Internet Opportunity for Going Global

The Internet provides an opportunity to go global instantly and inexpensively. The rapid feedback from customers around the world allows companies to adjust their way of doing business to the local culture and language. For example, Nike has sixteen sales representatives in Argentina for 38 million people. Using the Internet allows stores anywhere in Latin America to place orders thereby leveraging the sales staff.

7. Old Strategy - Total Quality Management (TQM) Process

The TQM concept that Demming championed entails improving all of your business's quality processes. TQM is necessary, but must be augmented by Hammer's business process reengineering.

New Strategy - Continual Business Process Reengineering (BPR)

BPR entails the identification and replacement of a critical business process with a process that is dramatically improved. For BPR to succeed, you need to select the correct process, obtain top management support, change the people in the process, and have an IT infrastructure that is able to cut across functions.

Internet Opportunity for BPR

The Intranet/Internet provides the mechanism for implementing the new process, and often is the new process. The key feature of the Internet for BPR is the three-tiered, client/server architecture that allows continual change of the functionality tier to match the new business process.

Summary

Business survival today requires new and dynamic strategies. A key component to implementing all of these strategies is the Internet.

Reinventing Your Business

The gun manufacturer Colt might still be around if it had reinvented itself around its real business of sporting and recreational equipment; it could have bought a tennis products manufacturer, for example. Imagine being on the other side of the net from a Colt 45!

The business strategies of Chapter 2 are necessary for a business to survive today, but will not necessarily lead to success in the future. A business could follow every one of these strategies and still not be a viable corporation in three years. For example, the CIO for GE Capital told me that, based on what is available on the Internet, he has only five years to reinvent his company. He now believes that all of his products and services will be offered more efficiently on the Internet. To put this in perspective, GE Capital provides approximately 50% of the profits of GE, one of the largest and most successful companies in the world.

The impetus for reinventing a corporation can come from the positive foresight and vision of its leaders or from several nuclear strikes directed at that corporation. Examples of potential forces in today's world that would require reinvention include the following:

- **Government:** Around the world there has been a reduction in defense budgets. In Russia defense spending has fallen from 30% of GDP to 15%. In the United States budget cuts have reduced military spending from 8% of GDP to 4%. Similarly, European countries such as France have made drastic cuts in the aerospace industry. Every aerospace and defense company in the world must reinvent itself in order to survive.

- **Deregulation:** Massive deregulation has occurred around the world; especially in banking, insurance, telecommunications, and utilities. Companies that were once regulated are now deregulated. Deregulated companies must now pay attention to customers rather than regulatory agencies. They need to reinvent themselves by offering new services, making business transactions easier, and sustaining massive consolidation immediately in order to survive. (The 10,000 banks in the US today will probably consolidate to about 4,000 in the future.)

- **Privatization:** Privatization around the world is taking place as governments are selling off state-owned companies to raise cash or effect more efficiently run businesses; Argentina has privatized both of its telephone companies and all of its utilities; France, England, and Germany have privatized utilities and transportation. These are all new companies in new business environments; they have all been pushed out of their protective nests and need to reinvent themselves in order to fly.

- **Technological advances:** The semiconductor industry experienced a 60% drop in prices in the first quarter of 1996. Companies like Samsung must reinvent themselves to survive.

- **Market Forces:** The role of women in business has required traditional women's consumer product companies to reinvent themselves around the new woman of the '90s. Companies that failed to do so, such as Laura Ashley and Lord & Taylor, have suffered.

- **Political Events:** When the economies of Eastern Europe changed from communism to capitalism, it necessitated the reinvention of companies within Eastern Europe and has affected countries outside of this block. For example, Germany has traditionally been the economic engine of Europe. With the fall of communism in Eastern Europe, a vast supply of inexpensive, skilled labor became available. As a result, Germany has been outsourcing its manufacturing and production to these countries. In addition, the financial burden of reunification and the constraints of the Maasticht Treaty have combined to limit the growth of the German economy. This new business model requires Germany and the rest of Western Europe to reinvent themselves.

- **Changing Business Model:** The entire business model has changed for many countries around the world. For example, the opening of markets in South Korea, Argentina, and Brazil, has forced companies in these countries to reinvent the way that they conduct business. Brazil had a business

25

model that closed its home market to protect the local industries. Today, in order for Brazilian companies to enter foreign markets, they have had to open their markets to foreign companies. Even if Brazilian companies do not go global, their customers will be exposed to global quality, and will not settle for less. Therefore, Brazilian corporations need to reinvent themselves for the future in global markets. That is, meet the competition on its own turf before it comes into yours.

- **Stabilization of currency:** In the past five years many countries have taken drastic and innovative steps to stop rampant inflation; Argentina guaranteed the peso relative to the dollar; Brazil indexed all its products and services. These measures have been enormously successful in reducing inflation to essentially zero. Good, right? Not if you're a bank. Last year's business model of banks in these countries was to make money on this inflation. Banks must reinvent themselves around this new business model and get the IT infrastructure in place to support it.

- **Legal:** New legislation such as the potential change to the Glass-Stiegel Act, allowing banks to sell insurance in the US, and allowing telecommunications companies to sell data services in Argentina will force many companies to reinvent themselves immediately.

Reinventing Your Business

The market, the competitive environment, and the Internet will force businesses to reinvent themselves. If you reinvent yourself, you live; if not you die. If you use the Internet, you live; if you don't, you die. You must reinvent your company now and in the future. How do you do it and what are the pitfalls? First, several long-held corporate tenets must be discarded:

- *A stable organization is good.* Wrong. To reinvent yourself, you must destabilize every aspect of the organization.

- *Managers should seek careers.* Wrong. They should seek to be legends.

- *We must manage to the bottom line.* Wrong. We must manage to the future.

- *We must continually downsize.* Wrong. You cannot starve yourself to success.

- *We must have a firm five-year plan.* Wrong. We must be opportunistic.

The process of continually reinventing your organization is not easy. It is an art implemented with hard work. It requires visionary leadership from the very top of the organization. This book provides a framework for the process and an implementation infrastructure: the Internet.

There are three starting points to achieve a successful reinvention.

1. Leverage Your Core Business

Find new areas based on your current operations. One process is to have a meeting with your senior people, as well as outside advisors. Start by analyzing what your business is, what it is good at, and then how it can be leveraged into future growing markets. This is a process which resonates well with Western cultures. Kodak has reinvented itself by leveraging its core competency in chemical photography into digital photography. Unisys has attempted to reinvent itself by leveraging its core competency in computer expertise into the systems-integration business. DHL's chairman took his senior management on a retreat with the purpose of reinventing the company for the future. They agreed that their core business capabilities of delivering packages anywhere in the world could be leveraged into outsourcing customer logistic systems; that is, keeping parts for service centers globally.

2. Reinvent Into Entirely New Business Markets

Another starting point is to find a new business in an attractive market. The corporation's senior management can look at new markets and new opportunities in the world, regardless of its current business. For example, Tong Yang is one of the largest cement companies in South Korea. Its chairman decided that financial services would be an important business area with potential growth in South Korea. He began buying financial services companies. Today, Tong Yang is an important financial services company in South Korea; and still one of the largest cement companies.

The strategy of entering a new business area works well in Eastern cultures. One reason is that a major barrier to entry in the East is capital. If a company has capital, it can buy its way into a new business, while potential competitors with less capital are excluded. In the West, capital is relatively easy to acquire; instead, ideas and management tend to be the major barriers to entry.

3. Expand Your Boundaries

Companies that reinvent themselves start with moving their business boundaries, looking at their basic charter, and expanding a boundary into new adjacent business areas. Microsoft's business territory, as defined by its boundaries, was the desktop. For its first 20 years Microsoft focused on owning the desktop computing niche; MS-DOS, Windows, and PC applications defined the environment. It had developed a brilliant strategy of opening up its operating system and leasing or giving basic software to application developers. These developers flocked to MS-DOS and Windows thereby killing other operating systems such as Macintosh.

By 1996 Microsoft was the target of several nuclear attacks from IBM, the US Justice Department, and a ground-zero hit by Netscape and the Internet.

In response, Microsoft continually reinvented itself in stages. It expanded a boundary from the desktop into the enterprise with NT, used a joint venture with NBC to expand into entertainment, partnered with Visa International to expand into banking; and, most recently, in an all out effort, reinvented itself to expand into the Internet.

Another example is Samsung that recently visited CTG to reinvent itself. It started by extending its core businesses of retail, finance, and insurance into global markets via the Internet.

Summary

Through vision and leadership, a CEO acting alone, an executive group acting together, or a collection of inside and outside people can drive the process of reinventing an entire business. If you wait, a nuclear attack on your business will force you to reinvent yourself; that is, if you are still alive. Corporations must continually reinvent themselves to survive and succeed in the future.

Part 2

Internet Revolution

4

Business and Technology Together At Last

The Internet provides a quantum leap of progress in the integration of business strategy and information technology. Although there has been an information explosion on the Internet, companies and people still hold a limited view of its potential. Today's use of the Internet is on the scale of using laser technology solely as a three-hole paper punch. In this chapter, we will examine how the Internet is currently being used and how it can better be utilized. More importantly, we will focus on how to use the Internet to enhance all aspects of your business.

What is the Internet? As has been said, fundamentally, it is two things:

- A standards-based physical communications network that runs over existing communications media

- A collection of basic software standards that includes email, file transfer protocols, browsers, web software; and a host of applications and data

The Internet is global; accessible in every country in the world. It is also robust; its infrastructure and protocols were originally designed to withstand a nuclear attack. Lastly, it is inexpensive, not because it is subsidized, as is commonly believed; rather, because

Internet pricing operates under a different premise than current telephone-pricing models. For example, traditional long-distance telephone calls are charged by the mile and by the minute. When accessing the Internet, no matter where in the world, the server machine is located, you usually just pay for a local telephone call to your Internet access provider along with your fixed access charge.

The Evolution of Business on the Internet

Figure 4-1 shows the evolution of the business use of the Internet, with the first uses being global email and general access to company information. The dates approximate the beginning of general industrial-strength use. By 1993 there was widespread use of the Internet for decision-support systems in such areas as stock market analysis. Facilities for sharing information were generally available by 1995. However, support tools for business transactions generally were not available for industrial-strength use by 1996. That is, an Internet user could access a web site to get information about the company, but was told to telephone or fax orders to that company. With the advent of plug-ins, ActiveX and Java applets, full business on the web is just beginning. In the future, tools that support workflow (business-to-business transactions) and widely accessible multimedia will emerge.

Figure 4-1: Internet Business Evolution Framework

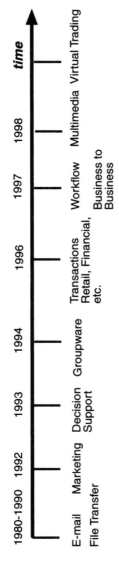

Mail and File Transfer

Most of the traffic on the Internet has been email and file transfers. Programs such as Gopher can search Internet sites for information. These programs, however, were awkward and hard for nontechnical people to use. With the advent of easier search engines and web browsers, finding information has become much easier; and has fueled the use of the Internet as a marketing tool.

Marketing

Organizations started putting information about their business and services on web sites that could be accessed over the Internet. The basic idea was that a user could search for sites by key words to find an associated organization's home page. The information about the company and its products and services was formatted on the home page and subsequent web pages. These web pages were stored on a web server in a new language, HyperText Markup Language (HTML), coupled with an Internet protocol, HyperText Transfer Protocol (HTTP), accessed by a search engine, and displayed on a client machine with an Internet browser. This web of information introduced a new concept called the World Wide Web. The World Wide Web and all the associated standard software is called the web. At present, the major business use of the web is marketing.

The Internet for Advertising

Figure 4-2 shows Samsung's home page. Clicking on products will load another web page of information about the top-10 biggest-selling items. Clicking on the various products gives information about each. Users cannot order the products via this web page. They must activate email, make a telephone call, or fax an order form. Like most companies, Samsung does not allow ordering, shipping, insuring, or financing of its products via the Internet. As it stands, the function of most web sites is product and company advertising; not performing business transactions.

Figure 4-2: Samsung's Homepage - Advertising on the Internet

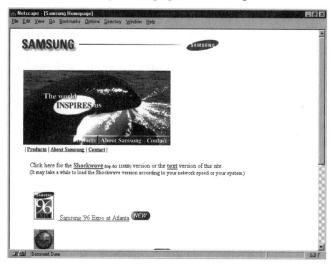

Decision Support Systems

The web and the Internet have evolved further with the advent of interactive web sites. Using the Internet and the resources afforded by the web can help with information on what stock to buy, where to go on vacation, or which college to attend. Hence, the Internet can act as a decision support systems (DSS).

Previously, only professional brokers and financial professionals had access, through proprietary applications and networks (e.g., Micrognosis and Quicktram), to company information, historical stock data, news, and financial reports that would support informed buying decisions on the stock market. In the past, only travel agents had up-to-the-minute information about resorts and travel options. Today, anyone with an Internet connection can access such information. Figure 4-3 shows MIT's StockMaster stock history and information web site. From this site you can obtain stock prices and historical trends free of charge to allow more informed purchasing decisions.

Figure 4-3: StockMaster: DSS on the Internet

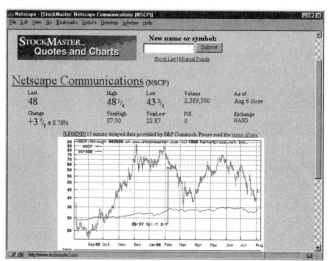

Many interesting sites with decision-support applications are mentioned in most books on the Internet. But today most of these sites all share a fundamental deficiency; the site only provides information; not complete business transactions. For example, many sites offer weather reports, tide tables, and beach and water conditions. Together with hotel listings, you could plan an entire vacation. But since the business transaction functions are unavailable, the user cannot register in the hotel or make a train reservation. Most of the literature today neglects to explain how to conduct business transactions over the Internet.

Groupware

Groupware is a class of software and activities that supports collaboration among individuals. Many organizations have groupware environments to bring design/development staffs around the world together on the same CAD object, spreadsheet, or document. The Internet's infrastructure can do the connectivity, and software packages such as Netscape's CoolTalk, Microsoft's NetMeeting, or Lotus Notes can enable such collaboration.

Even with these collaborative tools, though, today's users are still limited in their efforts to conduct robust business on the Internet. For example, after the new spreadsheet is formulated in a collaborative means and all parties agree on its numbers, there is no mechanism to load these numbers into the corporation's financial computers or manufacturing systems. The shared-document paradigm does not extend to the enterprise; hence, the business process remains incomplete.

Revolution on the Internet - Business Transactions

The previous examples represent how business is being conducted on the Internet today. As a bare minimum, your organization must be at this level to compete effectively. What has been discussed is an evolution of the use of Internet technology. Web sites, decision support systems, and groupware are already commonly used. However, use of the web for transactions facilitates a dramatic business revolution that will destroy all of the old business procedures. It will redraw all the boundaries of business and redefine the players: your partners, your distributors, your competitors, and even your doctor. It will allow you to conduct your business in an entirely different way: interactively, inexpensively, and in realtime. Some of these players will thrive; others will be destroyed.

If you are to take advantage of business on the web, two things must happen: First, executives need to know what business functions the Internet can perform and incorporate those functions into their business. Second, the technical people and contractors must understand and use the basic technology and architecture that makes business on the Internet possible. The next section briefly addresses this basic technology and architecture. Chapters 7 and 8 contain a more detailed discussion of technology.

Companies can now conduct the core businesses of billing, shipping, ordering, advertising, and purchasing on the Internet. This discussion will extend to all businesses, large or small; in all sectors, including retail, health, manufacturing, education, government, banking, insurance, and trading. The underlying core technologies to support such transactions include the web browsers, security, transaction processing, client-building tools, connectivity-building tools, network-management tools, prepackaged business objects for accessing legacy applications, and prepackaged business components for financing, shipping, and insuring. Again Chapters 7 and 8 discusses these technologies in further detail.

Internet Technology

The Internet is based on a three-tiered, client/server architecture. Using the World Wide Web portion of the Internet, the presentation layer may be any browser; most popular are Netscape's Navigator or Microsoft's Internet Explorer. The middle layers contain application software for connectivity to other systems, application functionality, network management, and emerging basic business components. The middle layer also contains web servers for maintaining web pages written in HTML. The data layer may be a database, legacy system, or software package, such as SAP, Baan, or PeopleSoft.

With the present Internet architecture and infrastructure, a user in Hong Kong can place an order in a legacy system in New York. For this to work, your web page must contain software components that directly access servers in the middle layer. These new visual software components in a web page can access functionality modules that can access legacy systems anywhere in the world. An order may be initiated from a web client in Paris to a legacy system of a retailer in London and financed through underwriters in Seoul.

Business Transactions on the Web

With these new business components, the Internet forms a far-reaching communications infrastructure that can perform all the basic functions of business such as ordering, shipping, and financing. Companies can then build or customize business components, or use

ones that already exist. Organizations have already built
and now offer components for financing, insuring, shipping, and advertising. These business components can
be activated from any web page.

This book is not to meant to be a technical
manual for developing and implementing these systems; it will refer you to corporations currently building Internet business transaction solutions such as HP,
c-bridge, or I-Cube, or the educational programs of
Cambridge Technology Group. Rather, this book is
meant to show how to use the Internet to support a
business reinvention strategy. It is important to note,
however, that since many technologies are not well
known, there is danger in choosing the wrong partner
to implement your Internet business; beware of
proprietary vendors.

Workflow on the Web

Workflow refers to a set of actions that users take to
accomplish tasks. The Internet not only facilitates work
between businesses, it can revolutionize the business
ecostructure of such transactions. An example of workflow is a customer placing an order for an automobile.
In the near future, the car may be ordered from General
Motors via an Internet terminal, credit may be checked
by GE Capital, insurance provided by Samsung, and
vehicle registration provided by the local Department of
Motor Vehicles.

Such a workflow transaction is often termed relaxed
computing. The entire workflow may be completed in

seconds if all of the processes proceed without the need of special handling; or days if human intervention is needed to perform a special task such as face-to-face negotiation for a customer with a bad credit rating. The Internet provides the physical network to connect these disparate sites, the software infrastructure to ensure the completion of transactions, and the means to monitor transactions.

Note that some software packages, such as SAP, Baan or PeopleSoft, presently offer workflow features. Such workflow, however, is often confined to monitoring processes within their packages. There are emerging workflow tools that support transactions among heterogeneous companies and IT infrastructures such as NEC's workflow engine.

Multimedia

As it develops in the future, multimedia will greatly enhance the way that business will be conducted. For example, videoconferencing that once cost $20,000 a seat can now cost as little as $30 a seat with the Internet. The business benefits of this technology will include lower travel cost, more efficient business transactions, and better personal interaction with the customer. These multimedia technologies, however, are just beginning to be ready for robust, high-transaction, enterprise computing. The technical breakthroughs that will make multimedia more viable include:

- Higher-bandwidth physical media

- Understanding the basis of human interactions
- Improvements in graphic software and high-speed hardware
- Cost reduction in computing
- Proxy server technology

There are several outstanding research institutions that the reader may want to follow, including the MIT Media Laboratory, which continues to be the leader in this promising field.

Summary

Business on the Internet is here today! Where do you start if you want to take your business to the World Wide Web? The next three chapters answer this question.

5

Reinventing the Corporation on the Internet

Senior management and you have decided to incorporate business transactions over the Internet into your core business strategy. So where and how do you start? Is there a road map for the Internet? First, two terms need to be clarified: Internet and a subset of the Internet called the World Wide Web. The Internet supports many communication protocols for email messaging, file transfers, applications, and data. As stated, the Internet consists of a physical network using TCP/IP standards; and a set of software standards, data, and applications. The web is a subset of these software standards, data, and applications; in general it is all the functions that can be accessed by a browser. This book focuses on extending business processes primarily using the web. This chapter outlines five steps in this process:

- Construct or obtain a web site.

- Enhance your web site's functionality.

- Fix your internal systems.

- Extend your legacy systems.

- Conduct business-to-business transactions.

These steps end with reinventing your business on the Internet.

Step 1: Construct or obtain a web site

The architecture for a web site is depicted as Step 1 in Figure 5-1 and consists of a web server machine to maintain the web pages and client machines running browsers to access the pages.

Figure 5-1: Architecture for expanding a web site for business

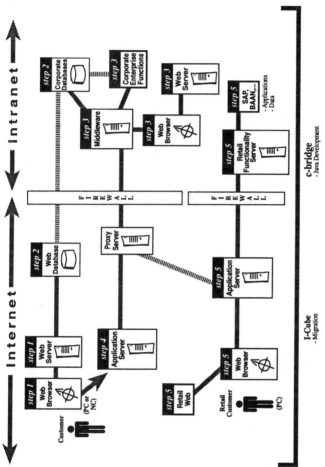

If you do not have a web site, get one. It can be designed and implemented in days at low cost. Web sites do not necessarily need to be developed by your staff. There are local Internet service hosts that can develop and maintain corporate web sites for you. Companies like USWeb provide a global network of professional web development, online marketing, and web site management. This section will describe how to add value by increasing business functionality.

In the following example, this five-step implementation methodology is used to extend the functionality of the web site of a bank. The example accomplishes the bank's goal of customer/business functions on the web. Figure 5-1 shows the architectural growth of all five steps in the example.

Step 2: Enhance your Web Site

NationsBank, the fourth largest bank in the US, is used for this example. Figure 5-2 depicts the home page of NationsBank. Clicking on any of the headings gives information about the bank. (Note that the primary purpose of this web page is to give information about the bank.) The major use of the web today is to advertise and market a company and its products. Figure 5-1 shows the conceptual configuration of Step 1 in the portion where the users are the bank's customers.

Figure 5-2: NationsBank's Homepage

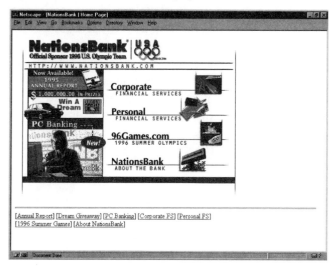

The web browser resides on the user's PC while the web pages reside on the bank's servers. This is where NationsBank stands today. All of the connections of Figure 5-1 do not yet exist.

Let's take this example to business transactions on the web. The functionality of the web site has been extended to allow a user to get personalized information. Here, the bank will add the ability to check the status of a customer's account; such as checking, savings, mortgage, or trust. With this feature, customers can get personalized information. Presently the customer information for the bank is maintained in the corporate database, but not accessible to web users. As depicted in Step 2 of Figure 5-1, activate a web site so users can access the web database. In the background, corporate data may be downloaded and updated periodically to the web server's data base, which is accessible by web clients. Note that this step does not give access directly to the corporate systems, only the mirrored data on the web server. Several packages, such as dbWeb, can be used to create and maintain web interfaces to databases, and provide a mechanism for simple queries to be performed from a browser. Web databases can contain any information that a customer may want, such as current product offerings, including special package deals and large-quantity discounts.

Step 3: Fix your Internal Systems

Intranet: Changing Business Strategies

Use the standards and the architecture of the Internet to rebuild your internal IT to support changes in today's business strategies. Create an Intranet using Internet standards including a web browser interface, TCP/IP, and three-tiered architecture. Divide your internal IT applications into separate entities: presentation, functionality, and data. This architecture allows for growth of the internal application without a major overhaul, and future improvements without having to shut down the whole system.

Intranet: Systems Management

Furthermore, having a three-tiered system with a web interface solves such issues as version control since the web browser interactively downloads web pages, applets, and weblets; the web server controls client application versions. Version control and client software updates can be maintained on a single machine as a function of the Internet infrastructure. All the communication between the presentation, functionality, and data occurs via the standard Internet protocol of TCP/IP.

Intranet: Prepare for the Internet

Building an Intranet architecture offers tremendous business benefits to your organization by integrating internal systems. Such an architecture would bring the internal organization all the tools and technical advances of the Internet, while restricting access from the outside. Then, if management decides to extend access to the world via the web, you can extend the web interface to Internet users and add appropriate security.

Intranet: Fix the Year 2000 Problem

Senior management is faced with an IT problem: the year 2000. The year 2000 problem stems from the fact that many old applications, especially those running on mainframes, reserved only two digits for the year field. When the year 2000 comes, '04 could be interpreted as 1904 or 2004. This has disastrous financial implications for certain calculations such as interest rates or amortization. Since a major rewrite will have to take place, be sure to rewrite all the programs with the correct Internet architecture that will solve the year 2000 problem and prepare your organization for the future on the Internet.

The Second Industrial Revolution

Intranet: Rearchitecting your IT

To show how internal operations are improved with an Intranet solution, reconsider the bank case. The current IT architecture of most banks is organized by product; hence, it is very difficult to get a complete view of the customer. In most banks around the world, different systems are used for each product offered, and these systems are not joined. An Intranet solution would solve this problem.

As described in the previous sections, there are two possible solutions:

1. Rewrite all applications in a three-tiered, client/server architecture. The portion of Figure 5-1 labeled Step 3 depicts this architecture.
2. Use the surround architecture leaving the legacy systems in place and adding a functionality layer in front of them which would act as the gateway to the web browser.

Constructing an Intranet for your internal operations is potentially the most expensive of these five steps. It entails hardware, software, and user consultancy services. As one specific example, Wisconsin Power & Light (WP&L) had to reinvent the entire company because of the business forces of deregulation and the inability of its current IT architecture to respond. An example of this is the City of Janesville, Wisconsin, a WP&L customer. At present it receives 250 bills per month, and wants to receive only one. The solution was to build an Intranet infrastructure.

WP&L's customer-service representatives can now look at all aspects of a customer-service contract, including billing information, usage, and rate structure. Working with a service representative, the customer can run a business more efficiently by taking advantage of better decision support from WP&L.

Step 4: Extend your Legacy Systems

This step describes how to conduct business transactions on the Internet. Customers anywhere in the world can withdraw money, make deposits, and check account balances. The bank can allow its customers the added value of doing business on the web. Step 4 in Figure 5-1 shows the architecture.

Extend your existing IT applications to the web: have your customers, suppliers, and partners access your internal system via the Internet. For example, those organizations that have implemented an enterprise resource planning system (ERP) such as Baan, SAP, Oracle, or PeopleSoft have a workable backbone for their internal operations.

A critical business strategy question often asked is, "If my organization has purchased one of these integrated applications, how can I get a competitive advantage when many competitors have the same system?" How can you differentiate your use of SAP from your competitors'? The Internet is your answer. Extend these systems to your customers, suppliers, or partners; and offer a tremendous strategic advantage before your competitors do.

To allow these business transactions to be executed, additional application servers are required to act as the gateway between the client and the corporate enterprise for each of the added business functions. An application server manages the actual web application whereas the web server manages access to the web page. A web server is accessible to the public and shouldn't have access to corporate systems. Also, since the web server is responsible for serving web pages, it shouldn't be further encumbered with running web applications. Now the users can directly enter orders; or update personal information or preferences. Tools for developing these application servers include Active Software's ActiveWeb. Tools for allowing client access to these servers include inserting Java applets, ActiveXs, and plug-ins into web pages using Microsoft and Symantec tools.

Step 5: Conduct Business to Business Transactions

The next step makes web-enabled business functions available to businesses with which a company has partnered. These business functions allow users of your web page to initiate business-to-business transactions such as coordination of materials planning, goods ordering, or logistics. A three-tiered Intranet system can customize business functions to connect to other systems not in the organization.

For example, the bank may further reinvent itself by partnering with a retail outlet as shown at the bottom of Figure 5-1; customers ordering from the retail systems can get financing from the bank. Customers using such a system can seamlessly do business with each party. Over the Internet, the retail company and bank can transparently process, order, and complete payment. Tools for designing and conducting such business-to-business Internet applications include the NEC workflow engine.

The bottom line is simply this: If you do not have the capability to run your business over the Internet, you will not be a player in the future business world. Your company will die.

Summary

No matter what starting point is applicable to your business, start and start now. Implementing an Internet strategy is no longer optional, it is imperative!

6

Business Examples on the Internet

Many senior managers may be skeptical of being the first to do business on the Internet. As the saying goes:

"The earliest Christians got the freshest lions."

So who else is doing business on the web? What are industrial examples? What were their benefits?

The purpose here is to discuss several businesses that were reinvented using the Internet. While we have chosen representative cases from a spectrum of industries, including telecommunications, retail, manufacturing, and utilities, the strategies in this book will be customized as necessary. With each case, the purpose is to explain the business use of the Internet and the internal architecture necessary to support online business transactions. You may mix and match relevant features as they apply to your business.

In all cases, senior management met with CTG's staff to focus on reinventing their business on the Internet. A pilot system was then constructed. Each case was implemented using the methodologies in Chapter 5.

Note, these systems are pilots; not prototypes or production systems. A prototype is a fake system that is not scalable; it exists solely on a PC with no connections to real systems or data. A production system is a fully functional, scaled system. A pilot connects to real systems and data, and is scalable. The only difference between a pilot and a production systems is that the pilot has not yet been fully deployed.

Case 1 - Telephone Company

The CTG team developed this business case and pilot application for a major North American telephone company. The president of this company said CTG could talk about the application in this book but, for strategic business reasons, did not want the name of this company revealed. Singapore Telecom and TeleDenmark are adapting and implementing the template for this application. For the purpose of this case study, the book refers to the companies as Telephone Company (TC) and Telephone Company Mobility (TCM).

TC, a major telecommunications company in North America, faces deregulation and foreign competitive pressure. TC's management decided to reinvent itself by leveraging its core business of telecommunications expertise to the new business of mobile phones. It established TCM and has operated it without the use of the Internet. As a result, costs have been higher than necessary and customer satisfaction lower than acceptable.

TCM is the cellular division of TC. It has 65% of the market share and annually generates $250 million in revenue. The process of purchasing, financing, and activating a telephone for home or business formerly took up to two days; the process spans three distinct organizations: the dealer, TCM, and the credit bureau. With its old systems, TCM was unable to manage across the entire process. Without implementing the new ordering process on the Internet, the customer and dealer start the process by filling out an application, a process that can take up to 30 minutes. The dealer then calls or faxes the information to TCM where it is sent to the credit bureau. If the credit check fails, the information is returned to the credit representative, who then determines the appropriate action, such as rejecting the application or negotiating a deposit amount needed before activation. The outcome of this process is then communicated to the dealer via telephone or fax.

Business Case

In addition to the unnecessarily lengthy process, the activation cost to TCM for one mobile phone is $250 for the phone, $200 commission given to the dealer for each phone sold; and $100 for TCM's internal installation and administrative costs. TCM's business model is to give the phone to the customer and recoup costs and profit from service and phone charges. That is, they invest $550 per activation before receiving any revenue from that activation. Thus, the key challenge is to devise an Internet solution that can reduce commission cost and activate the phone more quickly, allowing TCM to begin earning on service and phone charges sooner. Another quantifiable benefit is the ability to cross-sell with user profiles.

Business Benefits

TCM immediately noted several quantifiable benefits from the implementation of this Internet solution. Since the new process required less dealer effort, TCM was able to reduce the commission rate from $200 to $100 per activation. With approximately 96,000 activations per year, the immediate cost savings was $9.6 million. In most cases, the implementation of this new process allows TCM to activate a new service while the customer is standing in front of the dealer. On average, this is two days earlier than the old process, leading to the additional revenues associated with service and usage charges. In addition, this faster activation leads to a higher level of customer satisfaction, which inevitably leads to a higher rate of customer retention, according to Drucker.

Let us examine how reinventing TCM with the Internet pilot system can dramatically facilitated doing business.

Workflow Business

Workflow, a new concept in Internet use, was used to implement this new sales, service, and activation process. This workflow technology is not limited to workflow within one organization or within one software application. It enables many disparate applications and environments to work together. Workflow between companies and organizations means that the initiation of a transaction results in the triggering of an entire process that may involve actions by several entities, both manual and automated. As stated before, the term relaxed computing is often used to describe this process. Figure 6-1 depicts the flow and interaction of all the processes initiated by a customer arriving at a store. The first station depicts the functions of the dealer, the middle and lower right the functions of TC, and the bottom left the functions of the credit bureau. Since each organization has different systems, timetables, and coordination, workflow was helpful to implement the new processes. Furthermore, workflow technology automates reimplementing to accommodate changes to the process.

Figure 6-1: TC Workflow Diagram

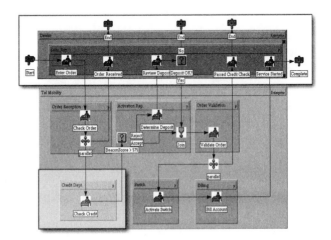

Starting at the top of Figure 6-1, a customer order is entered via fax or telephone to TCM. The order is checked and sent to the credit department and, if approved, a message is sent to begin the activation. If rejected, a negotiation takes place requiring additional actions such as security deposits.

Workflow Technology

From a technology vantage point, there are two parts to this workflow system: the workflow editor and the workflow engine. The workflow editor, whose output is depicted in Figure 6-1, specifies the relationship of processes, functions, the flow of actions, and the underlying corporate objectives. The workflow engine conducts the activation of each object within the Internet as specified by the editor. Using advanced workflow technology, such as that provided by NEC, changes to the workflow editor are immediately implemented by the workflow engine.

A workflow engine used as an application server on the Internet adds another dimension to the ability to deliver business solutions: it provides the backbone for routing the components so that users can participate at various stages of the process, even if they are in different physical locations. The workflow engine connects multiple disparate systems into a coherent business process, and promotes the idea of reusing application components in different business scenarios. For example, you may have a billing component which you need to use in your expense report, as well as your payroll process. All Internet business processes can be built within this framework of component-based workflow.

Telephone Company's Implementation

This section shows a customer/dealer interaction. Each of TCM's dealers will have a PC with Netscape that accesses the appropriate business components inside each solution. Table 2 shows TCM's corporate facts and application goals. Figure 6-2 depicts the three-tiered architecture of TCM's Internet application.

TABLE 2. *Corporate Facts and Goals of TC*

Organization Facts:	Important Processes:
• TC Cellular provider	• Order Entry
• 65% Market Share	• Credit Check
• $250 million annual revenue	• Switch Activation
• Parent TC $9 billion	• Dealer Notification
	• Billing Update

Goals:
• Reduce Cost
• Increase Sales

Critical Success Factors:	Users of System:
• Customer-Focus	• Dealers
• Provide dealers with fast, easy-to-use electronic delivery method	• Activations/Credit Reps
• Combination of automatic and human factors	• Managers

Figure 6-2: TCM/Dealers/Customers/Multiple phone ordering

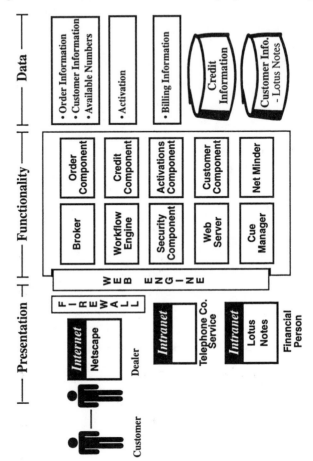

A customer visiting a store requests a mobile phone from a dealer. The dealer activates the Internet business application from the Netscape logon screen in Figure 6-3. Only authorized dealers with an assigned password can access the system. The dealer then sees the work list shown in Figure 6-4 displaying all the items that need to be processed and their current status. The added value of this realtime work list is that the dealer is constantly informed of the status of a customer order, wherever it is in the workflow process; and can, in turn, keep the customer aware of the status.

Figure 6-3: Logon component in Netscape page

Figure 6-4: Dealer Work List

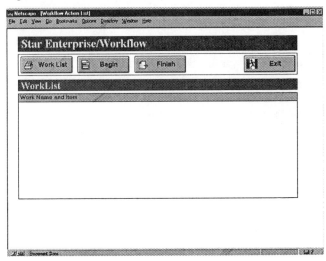

Figure 6-5 shows the entry of billing and credit information. The contents of this screen is then routed to the credit bureau for approval. If the customer's credit is automatically accepted; no interaction is needed. If a risky credit rating turns up, then negotiation and recommendation occur; a deposit may be required. See Figure 6-6.

Figure 6-5: Billing and credit information

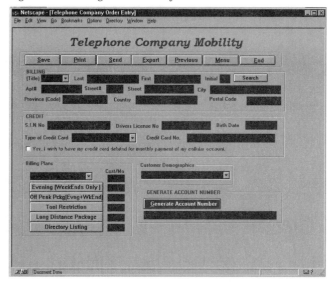

Figure 6-6: Credit rating, deposit required

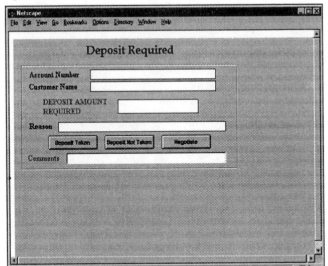

Once an order is placed, the workflow engine takes care of the communication between the credit bureau and the dealer, notifying the dealer of the current status of the process. This information can then be passed on to the customer, providing faster and more satisfactory sales support.

Figure 6-7 depicts the work list showing how this particular customer's order has been filled. Implementing this new process on the Internet provides customers of TCM with phone activations in just minutes and dealers with up-to-date status information of the order to support the sales process.

Figure 6-7: Worklist with completed order

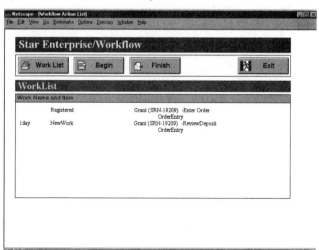

Management Benefits

In addition to increased customer satisfaction, this online system allows managers to track orders through the process and pinpoint the bottlenecks and break points in that process. Since most of the employees of TCM are cross-trained, this information allows a dynamic reassignment of resources to problem areas.

Technical Benefits

Because the system uses the Internet, it does not require dedicated lines or an expensive network. The workflow engine brings the latest application components to the user each time they are needed. Since the components which are carried in the workflow are all stored in a central repository, the workflow engine han-

71

dles maintenance and version control of the software; any change in the repository will be reflected in the workflow process. Version control of the visual components is handled by the normal web infrastructure.

Furthermore, the open architecture supports many client platforms. Since these components can be ActiveX or Java applets, they will be accessible to virtually all users on the Internet, including all Windows platforms, UNIX, or Java machines.

Case 2 - Levi Strauss & Co.

Where can a retail company start? Where are the business benefits for reinventing the business to the Internet?

Levi Strauss & Co. apparel is a $6.5 billion company, employing more than 37,000 people. It currently has a well-designed and alluring web site with product lines, search capabilities, and apparel images. However, the present web site only provides marketing and advertising information; it does not allow ordering, financing, insuring, or shipping, directly over the Internet. The web sites of most retail companies contain such limited business functionality. Again, these sites were initially designed for advertising, not conducting business over the Internet. To implement the pilot system described next, Levi Strauss started at Step 2 of Chapter 5. This system allows Internet users to select, view, and order jeans with a custom fit.

Business Benefits

The business benefits include increased revenues through global access to Internet users, the possibility of cross-selling to its customers, and immediate and accurate feedback from customers. This information could be critical to decisions about specific products and product lines. Also, the user's ability to customize jeans allows for reduced inventories from just-in-time manufacturing.

Levi Strauss' Implementation

Table 3 overviews the organizational facts of Levi Strauss, its goals, and critical success factors.

TABLE 3. *Corporate Facts and Goals of Levi Strauss*

Organization Facts:	Important Processes:
• Manufacture, distribute, and market branded casual apparel	• Easy access to product information
• $6.8 billion sales	• Simple order process
• 37,000 employees	

Goals:	Users:
• Increase market share	• Anyone who wants to interact with Levi Strauss for products or services
• Close relationship with customers	• Manager

Critical Success Factors:
• Customer satisfaction
• Adapt to changing market

Figure 6-8 shows the architecture diagram of the Internet pilot that was implemented. The CTG team extended the functionality of Levi Strauss' enterprise legacy systems to the Internet, allowing the Internet user to do product ordering, billing, and shipping.

Figure 6-8: Architecture diagram: Levi Strauss &Co.

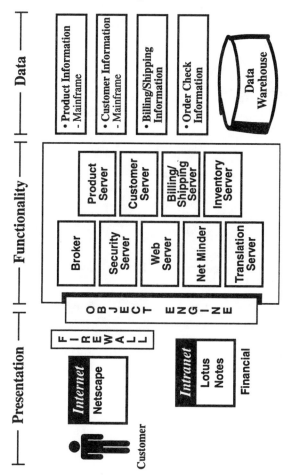

For this pilot application, Visual Basic 5 components were once again embedded in the existing Levi Strauss web site. Figure 6-9 is the logon screen with password and language-selection functionality. Note that the CTG did not need to write this component. Rather, it was selected from a repository of existing components as an example of reusable object technology.

Figure 6-9: Levi Strauss: logon component within homepage

A satisfactory logon uniquely activates the product-selection screen in Figure 6-10. The product list component accesses a server that retrieves the data from a CICS database using Open Environment Corporation's (OEC's) Entera technology. The customer clicks on a product number which activates a server that retrieves an image from a database. This image appears on this same screen. In the future, a video could be added to this screen presenting a better view of the apparel.

Figure 6-10: Product selection screen

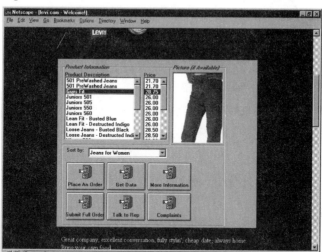

Another feature is the customer service/complaints button. The Internet will revolutionize the customer-service business. Text listing common complaints and solutions, and videos showing common installation procedures could be used in conjunction with videoconferencing to respond to customer complaints in real-time. This reinvented customer service would be more responsive and less costly than present methods.

Before submitting the order, users can input exact measurements, ensuring a customized fit of their jeans. As previously discussed, this functionality provides the added business value of reducing inventory and merchandise returns.

The payment, billing, and shipment methods are filled out in the screen in Figure 6-11. This function gives added value for the customer and Levi Strauss' business partners. The customer may choose any preferred method of payment allowing Levi Strauss to provide more business to its financial partners. The shipping can then be handled by specialized organizations, such as UPS if domestic; or DHL if global.

Figure 6-11: Credit, shipping, and billing form

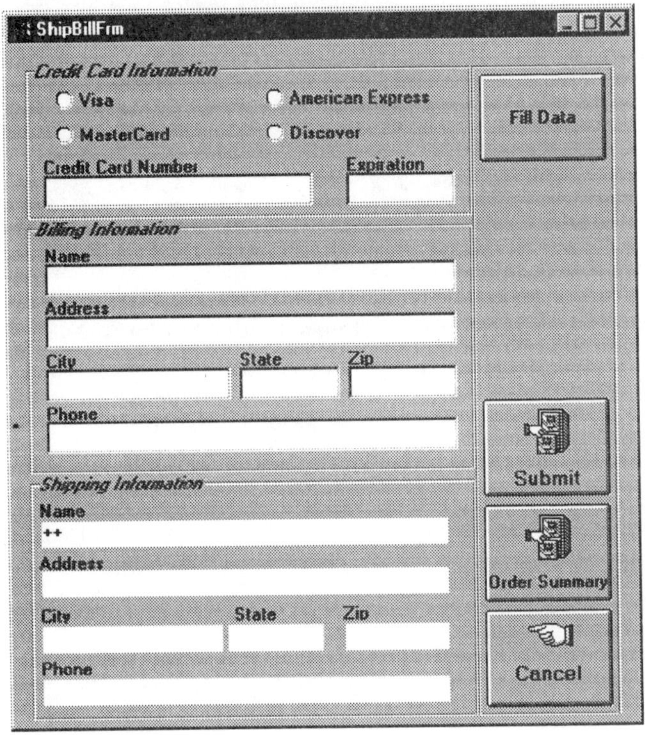

Case 3 - Companhia Siderurgica Nacional-(CSN) Brazil

I am a manufacturer. What added value can I give to my customer via the Internet? What additional revenue sources do I have? Are my customers a hidden market for selling other products?

CSN is a $2.6 billion manufacturer of flat steel products in Brazil, with a 45% market share. CSN sells its steel throughout Latin America and its goal is to dominate the region. The process of tracking an order was manual and took days to complete. Also, the information that was returned to the customer was hard to understand and filled with cryptic codes for the products and status of the order.

The system CTG created reinvented CSN on the Internet to provide its customers with an order-tracking capability. It was also decided that the customers of a Brazilian steel company might also be particularly good candidates for selling jeans and denim wear. Therefore, a business opportunity exists for combining Levi Strauss' web application with CSN's increasing revenues for both companies.

Business Benefits

CSN identified several business benefits of conducting business on the Internet. The first was increased customer satisfaction. Companies that rely on CSN steel found the system strategic to their processes. Information that used to take days to obtain now takes minutes. The system also reduces the number of duplicated orders that resulted from inaccurate or untimely information. The feedback and customer-receipt features allowed CSN to improve the shipping of its product. Furthermore, since the system is on the Internet, CSN now has a strategic system to expand its business throughout Latin America and to the rest of the world. Finally, the system allows for cross-selling and the associated profits from such endeavors.

CSN Implementation

CSN already had a good web site to obtain information about its products. To implement the Internet system, the CTG team again started at Step 2 of Chapter 5. As with every pilot application, the process began with analyzing the company's goals and critical success factors (Table 4).

TABLE 4. *Corporate Facts and Goals of Companhia Siderurgica Nacional*

Organization Facts:
- Steel production, flat products
- 45% Brazilian Market, 30% export
- 14,000 employees
- $2.6 US billion in revenue

Important Processes:
- Comprehensive views of all order information
- Easy access to information
- Feedback from customers

Goals:
- Customer satisfaction
- Increase market share
- Top quality service

Users:
- Customers

Critical Success Factors:
- Fast and efficient service
- Better knowledge of customer's needs

Figure 6-12 shows the architecture diagram for this system. The CTG team expanded the web site to allow business transactions on the Internet.

Figure 6-12: Companhia Siderurgica Nacional Steel Company Tracking Application

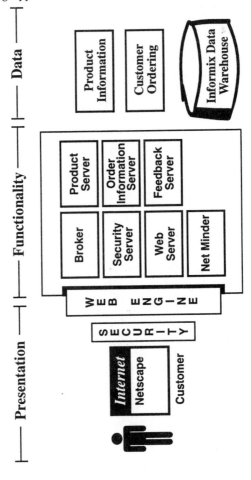

The logon component was reused and placed into Netscape in Figure 6-13. Once the logon is successfully completed, the user can choose which order to track by directly entering the order number or by selecting it from a list of retrieval orders associated with that customer. (See Figure 6-14.) Each time a new query is sent, the information is rapidly updated on the screen. Again, this is because the web page component directly activates a server that accesses the legacy system where all of this information resides. It is not repainting the whole page at each iteration or query request; this process is extremely tedious and would frustrate customers.

Figure 6-13: Logon component with password and language selection

Figure 6-14: Customer order-retrieval list

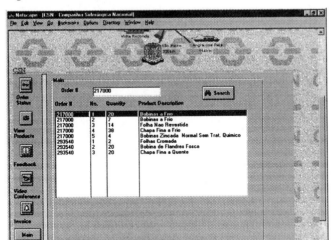

All the information pertaining to this order then appears on the next screen, as seen in Figure 6-15. Information that formerly required days to retrieve is now assembled immediately in a format that the customer finds useful. Since the system is on the Internet, it may be accessed anywhere in Latin America. Doing business over the Internet provides high value for low cost.

Figure 6-15: Order information

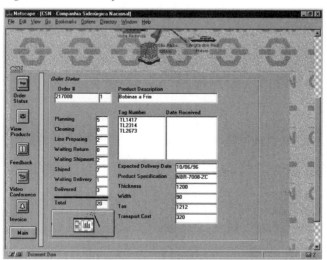

Another important feature for CSN's customers is the ability to check on outstanding invoices. To facilitate this process, users can start by selecting and viewing a product that they ordered (Figure 6-16). A list of invoices with the corresponding due dates then appears. This feature helps customers to avoid unnecessary delays in payment.

Figure 6-16: Product selection and viewing

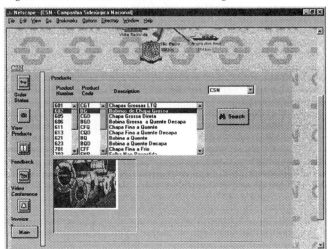

The last screen in Figure 6-17 allows CSN to improve delivery schedules. The customer fills out a form notifying CSN of a shipment's arrival. CSN uses several transport companies and has no means of knowing which ones provide more value-added to its customers. With this information, it can track the performance and customer satisfaction associated with the shipping companies.

Figure 6-17: Delivery schedules and customer feedback

Case 4 - American Packaging Corporation (APC)

APC is a medium-size company. Can it benefit from the Internet? Its senior management has no experience on the Internet whatsoever. Can it catch up? APC does have SAP, will it have to scrap it?

This case describes a pilot system developed for APC, a $200 million supplier of boxes, cartons, and packages to major consumer product companies, such as Cheerios cereal boxes for General Mills. Senior management has decided to spend considerable money reengineering internal processes and implementing an SAP system. How can they extend SAP to take advantage of the Internet?

87

Business Benefits

The business benefit of extending APC's systems to the Internet is adding capabilities that its competitors with SAP do not have; namely, customer access to ordering and tracking. Quantifiable business benefits include reduced internal time to process orders and the increased customer satisfaction associated with access to strategic manufacturing information.

APC Implementation

The CTG team started at Step 4 of Chapter 5 to take APC to the Internet. CTG extended APC's excellent internal system (SAP) for added business functions to a web site. Why not just take existing SAP screens and put them on the Internet? While these screens may be good for experienced technical users, they are difficult for untrained users. Furthermore, the screen-generating software of these application packages does not generally conform to Internet standards; hence, they are limited in functionality. For example, when was the last time you saw a video in a 3270 screen or a picture in a Baan screen?

APC wanted to create a system with order-tracking, timely feedback on orders, and ease of access and use for its Internet customers and its Intranet employees. Since it had no web site, the first step was to build one (a process that can be accomplished in a day). Figure 6-18 depicts the logon screen that activates the product selection. For each product selected, a picture appears showing the package (Figure 6-19).

Figure 6-18: American Packaging Systems' logon component within web page

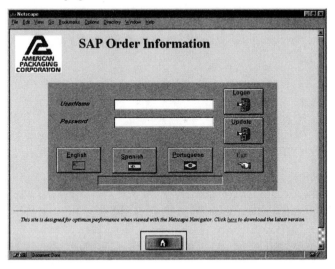

Figure 6-19: Product selection with picture and inventory quote

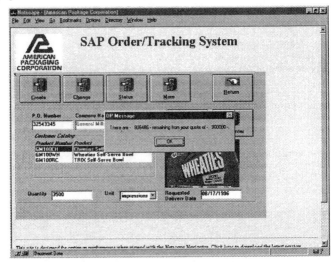

In the subsequent screens, the user would select an item to order and the quantity required, and the system would return with the total price information and the sales order number (Figure 6-20). The customer creates the order using a web screen; a server retrieves the information and updates the screen; and SAP handles the ordering, finance, controlling, materials management, and quote-management systems. All this processing occurs without requiring users to deal with the complex interfaces of the SAP systems.

Figure 6-20: Total price information and sales order number

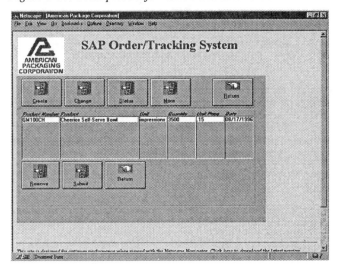

Organizations can implement such Internet application extensions in about three months, given the right IT infrastructure and top management support. The installation of the underlying SAP system may vary from six months to several years. The biggest factor in the implementations of packaged applications like SAP is the resolution of the business processes associated with the new application; not the package itself.

The implementation of this pilot system allows APC to extend its automated internal processes to the Internet. The added value associated with this system would allow APC to compete on a global scale and grow beyond its present $200 million in revenue.

Case 5 - Wisconsin Power & Light (WP&L)

What do I do if I must change everything in my business? What if deregulation makes my internal systems unsatisfactory for my new business?

WP&L is the dominant utilities company in the Midwest. Recent deregulation has forced it to focus on customer service and allowed it to buy two other utility companies. As one executive stated: "We used to focus on the customers who didn't pay; now we must focus on the customers who do pay." WP&L's legacy system could not support the business reinvention necessary in this new deregulated environment.

How could this utility reinvent itself? How about becoming the central utilities clearing house for the citizens of the state of Wisconsin and beyond? That is, all customer-service inquiries would be handled through WP& L. It would become the one-stop shop for all utilities: electricity, gas, water, and phone service. Its IT structure of disparate, inflexible systems that did not focus on the customer was inadequate for implementing this vision.

WP&L started at Step 3 of Chapter 5 to implement this system. That is, it developed a new client/server Intranet by migrating all of its legacy systems to Internet standards. In six months, with the help of a professional consulting organization (I-Cube), it migrated about 3.6 million lines of COBOL code into a three-tiered, client/server system, implemented a web browser interface, and used C++ functionality to tie into a relational database in a TCP/IP network.

The next step for WP&L is to extend the browser interface to the Internet, adding appropriate security to make all of the functionality of its systems accessible to anyone in the State of Wisconsin.

How will the reinvention of WP&L add value to the service that it provides its customers? With an expanded-function web page, customers would be able to check account information, pay bills, and order services automatically over the Internet. This capability would not only increase customer satisfaction, but reduce WP&L's administrative costs. The extension of these systems to the Internet could also be of value to other business. For example, from an Internet terminal, a manufacturing company in the state could determine its hourly electricity usage. That customer could then negotiate a deal over the Internet with WP&L to change the factory hours to a time when usage is lower, and receive a better rate structure.

Summary

Start—whether you are small or large, whether you have a homepage or a 3270 screen. Remember, whoever gets there first gets the best seat!

Part 3

Technology Framework

Internet Landscape

So, you have decided to use the Internet. Who are the players? What are the important technologies? What is a framework for understanding the products, services, and business opportunities around the Internet?

This chapter attempts to go where no one has gone before; to provide a road map for cyber-space—present and future.

Oil Business Revolution

By analogy, set the clock back to 1900. Inexpensive oil and the technologies to refine oil have been discovered. What are all the new industries that are going to emerge to support businesses that will use oil? There will be primary industries associated with the production, processing, and distribution of oil. There will be support industries that produce the tools for the end-user industries, including internal-combustion engines, jet engines, and automobile manufacturers. There will be the service industries, such as road builders and maintenance. Finally, there are the end-user industries: the airlines, trucking, railroads, and plastics manufacturers. This entire food-chain was made possible by oil and technologies to make it useful as a fuel.

Internet Business Revolution

Set the clock forward to the present. The Internet and the technologies to make it useful for business are a reality. Commerce in cyberspace is the beginning of another such revolution: the Internet revolution. The entire industrial food chain for the Internet is being created and the end-user businesses that will dominate the Internet are just beginning. You are now at this threshold. Do you want to be a player or a spectator?

Figure 7-1 again depicts the evolution of the use of the Internet. This chapter will only briefly discuss the technologies used before business transactions on the Internet; technologies such as email, file transfer mechanisms, groupware tools, and information gathering. While certainly important technologies, there are hundreds of books written on these subjects making an in-depth discussion here unnecessary. But what many have missed is that these technologies of email and groupware are converging to the web.

Figure 7-1: Internet Business Evolution - Framework

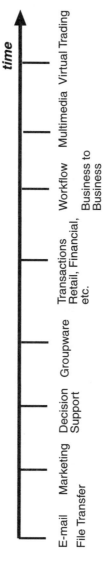

Email

Email has been considered a nonweb technology. In the past email used the physical network and transfer protocols, but has not used the web standards. However, email and the web are starting to merge. For example, Netscape has recently released Direct InBox that allows users to subscribe to desired specialized information. Direct InBox and others will not only email text, they will email all the web-enabled functions of HTML, applets, plug-ins, and forms. Your mail will come alive! Email is now sending web pages that are dynamic and interactive.

The web is driving the Internet standards, even for email. For example, the old email standards such as post office protocol (POP) are being replaced with the more encompassing standard of interactive mail access protocol (IMAP). IMAP takes advantage of the web architecture, only drawing appropriate portions of the email leaving the rest on the server. This allows for high performance and a thin client.

A word of caution for the business person. The conversion of technologies to the web standard necessitates that corporations not adopt clients, email, or groupware that are not web-compliant. Corporations that do not adopt web standards may find themselves at the gas station of life, with only a self-service pump.

The business benefits of email and browser technology converging include sending advertisements and mass target mailing with email. Other benefits include being able to send customers mail that can describe the product through pictures, voice or video; to interact with customer-service representatives; and to order, finance, and insure. The Internet will allow an entirely new method of census-taking, as a target person can interact with email received and return the appropriate information. Tedious and costly human-resources functions such as vacation requests will be facilitated, and interactive blueprints and designs can facilitate engineering decisions.

This chapter is about the technologies supporting the revolution on the Internet called the World Wide Web used for business transactions. It is this one small concept that has opened the floodgate, started the avalanche, and led to the volcanic eruption that is business on the Internet.

Framework

The framework here allows the reader to keep up with the technologies and the movement of the Internet revolution. However, the movement is progressing at warp speed. The framework will be constant. The players, products, winners, and losers will shift dramatically. The players and products here are merely a sample; they neither represent the best nor the worst. They are simply instances for your reference.

Roadmap To The Chapter

Figure 7-2 shows a framework for understanding the entire landscape of the web; a sample of its players, products, and opportunities. There are two audiences for this framework:

- Those who are interested in the competitive landscape of the web; that is, what products and services are being offered to support end-user businesses. This group should give the chapter a thorough reading. Again, in Internet time, these players will shift rapidly; however, this framework will not.

- Business executives who want to gain insight into what is possible and what support is available from the technologies for their businesses. This group should read the chapter focusing on the business benefits.

TABLE 5. *Internet Landscape Matrix*

HARDWARE	Country
Client PC's	
Toshiba	JPN
Compaq	USA
DEC	USA
Hardware 2000	UK
HP	USA
IBM	USA
Manstar (Custom PC's)	HKG
NEC (Satellite Pro)	JPN
Samsung (SENS 810)	KOR
Siemens Nixdorf BV (SCENIC Celcius)	NED
Client Network Computer	
Acorn (NetSurfer)	USA
Apple (Pippin)	USA
Bandai (Pippin)	JPN
JCC USA (iBox)	USA
NEC (Atom Net)	JPN
Oracle (NetVision)	USA
QNX (Explr1 Ex)	USA
SunRiver (Network Computer)	USA
Teknema (Easy Rider)	USA

TABLE 5. *Internet Landscape Matrix, (Continued)*

ViewCall (Web TV)	USA
WTTF (Welcome to the future)	USA
Client Personal Digital Assist. & Devices	
HP (Palmtop PC)	USA
Apple (Newton)	USA
Nokia (9000)	USA
Psion (3a)	USA
Sharp (Organizer)	USA
AT&T (Phone)	USA
Navio (TVs)	USA
Server Machines	
Compaq (Proliant)	USA
Digital Equipment (Alpha Servers)	USA
HP (K, D classes)	USA
IBM (SP2)	USA
ICE (ICE Board)	USA
Marathon (Fault Tolerant)	USA
Peripheral Technology International Ltd.	UK
SGI (Challenge Server)	USA
Sun (Netra NFS Server)	USA
Communications Equipment	
Backbones/switches	
Lucent (ATM Switch)	USA
Madge (IELB)	USA
Hub/router/switch	
3Com (Transcend Framework)	USA
Ascend (MaxZoo Plus)	USA
Bay Networks (Bay Stack Stackable Hubs)	USA
Cabletron (SmartSwitch)	USA
C-Connect Ltd (New Media Live Wire Plus)	SUI
Cisco (Cisco PRO • CPA 900)	USA
Madge (Madge Collage 280 Workgroup ATM)	USA
NTT (Astrowink • E)	JPN
Modem Technologies	
C-Connect Ltd. (New Media NetSurfer 28.8)	SUI
DVSD, ISDN, Cable	
Elebra S/A (ED-3410I)	BRA
Hayes (Optima 288)	USA
AHome (Cable Modem)	USA
Microcom (SOLIS-L)	USA
Motorola (VoiceSURFR 28.8)	USA
NEC (6450 DSU/CSU)	JPN
Telebit (NetBlazer)	USA
U.S. Robotics (Total Control MP/8)	USA

TABLE 5. *Internet Landscape Matrix, (Continued)*

HP (modems)	USA
Internet Processors	
Java chips	USA
Intel (Pentium Pro)	USA
Motorola (Power PC)	USA
Sun (Ultra Java)	USA
Cabling	
Amp Inc. (Horizontal Cable)	USA
Corttaillod Cossonay Cable (FiberOptic Cabling)	SUI
Dow Corning (Fiber Optics)	USA
Sumitomo (Copper Cabling)	JPN
Database Machines & Legacy systems	
IBM (mainframes)	USA
Internet Device	
Sony (Web TV)	JPN
Multimedia	
Creative Technology, Ltd. (SoundBlaster Discovery)	SIN
SmartCards	
Landis & Gyr (Phonecards)	SUI
Switches	
Apcon Inc. (POWERSWITCH)	UK
Virtual Reality Hardware	
VARTEC (Virtual Research)	BEL
SOFTWARE	
Web Browser	
Netscape (Navigator)	USA
Mosaic (Mosaic)	USA
Microsoft (Explorer)	USA
Client Tools	
Borland (Latté)	USA
K&K Software (Serviceangebot)	GER
Metaphor (Internet Starter Kit)	BEL
Microsoft (FrontPage)	USA
Rogueware (J Factory)	USA
Ettl Software	AUT
HP (Depot/J)	USA
Sausage Software (Hot Dog)	AUS
Sun (Java Workshop)	USA
Spider (CGI Bin)	USA
InContext (site management)	USA
PowerSoft (NetImpact)	USA
WideSoft Sistemas	BRA

TABLE 5. *Internet Landscape Matrix, (Continued)*

Web Development Tools	
Oekosoft (Web Page Generator)	SUI
Datamind (Syntos-Tools)	SUI
The Virtual World Company (Virtual Reality)	SUI
Web IT (Kioskmanager)	GER
Korea.com	KOR
Interactive Execution Environments	
JavaSoft (Java)	USA
AT&T (Inferno)	USA
Microsoft (ActiveX)	USA
Voice Communications	
Vocaltec (iPhone)	USA
InforInter Active (Internet Call Manager)	CAN
Video Conferencing	
White Pine (CU-SeeMe)	USA
Search Engines/Agents	
Argos (Argos	BRA
Digital (Alta Vista)	USA
Facing Facts (SearchForm)	NED
First One Internet Consultants Ltd.(HK Internet S-Engine)	HKG
Lycos, Inc. (Lycos)	USA
Swiss Search (Swiss Search)	SUI
Internet Wines Pty Ltd.	AUS
Japan InterSEARCH	JPN
Yahoo! (Yahoo!)	USA
Opentext (LiveLink)	USA
Groupware	
Bittco Solutions (Co-Motion)	CAN
Informatique MTF SA (HYPERNET)	SUI
Info Wan (PageGate)	GER
Lotus (Notes)	USA
Netscape (Collabra)	USA
Brainstorm (HelpDesk)	USA
NEC (Star Enterprise)	JPN
Microsoft (NetMeeting)	USA
Web Servers and Tools	
Bruker (NMR Software Server)	GER
O'Reilly & Associates (WebServer)	USA
Netscape (Commerce, Communications ProxySer-ver)	USA
Connect (OneServer)	USA
NaviSoft/AOL (NaviServer)	USA
Open Market (WebServer, Secure WebServer)	USA

TABLE 5. *Internet Landscape Matrix, (Continued)*

SecureWare (Secure WebServer)	USA
Siemens Nixdorf BV (NetServe)	NED
Spyglass (Spyglass Server)	USA
Microsoft (Internet Information Server)	USA
Network Management	
HP (OpenView)	USA
Sun (Net Manager)	USA
Cambridge Tech. Ent. (Netminder)	USA
Security/Authentication	
Raptor (Eagle)	USA
C-Dilla (CD Secure 2)	UK
CheckPoint (FireWall-1)	USA
Versing	USA
Trusted Info Systems	USA
Enigma Logic	USA
CenterPoint (Web Authentication)	USA
Security Dynamics	USA
Siemens Nixdorf BV (NetSafe)	NED
Digital Pathways	USA
Transaction Processing	
Open Market	USA
Edify	USA
NTT TP Monitor	JPN
BEA	USA
Database Access Tools	
Microsoft (Access)	USA
Cognita Software (SQL Web)	BEL
Antares	USA
NTT (WebBase)	JPN
Application Software	
SAP Ag. (SAP)	GER
Baan Company NV (Baan IV)	NED
Multimedia	
Australian Micro Multimedia	AUS
Artsys (Sistemas Multimidia)	BRA
Video Server	
MCS (WebCam)	NED
Internet Gateway	
WebArt Design	UK
Virtual Reality	
VARTEC (WorldToolKit)	BEL
SERVICE	

TABLE 5. *Internet Landscape Matrix, (Continued)*

Internet Access Providers/Enablers

Abaconet	ARG
Alands Nattjanster	FIN
at-net	AUT
AUSNet Service Pty. Ltd.	AUS
BBN Planet	USA
BushNet	AUS
CalvaNet	FRA
CaribSurf	BAR
Colomsat S.A.	COL
CTC-Mundo	CHI
Cybernet.dk	DEN
Cyberville	SIN
Czech.Net	CZE
Daiichi (NiftyServe)	JPN
EcuaNet	ECU
EuNet	SUI
EuroConnect GmbH	GER
Grandworld Technology Ltd.	HKG
Greatwall Netcenter	CHI
Holland Online	NED
Info Match	CAN
Internet Interactive Japan (Archive Server)	JPN
Kornet	KOR
MCI	USA
Mistral Internet	UK
Nacamar	GER
Nornet	AUS
OEC SA	SUI
PC-VA	USA
SofiCom Communications	EGY
Systemec Internet Services	NED
Ultra BBS	BRA

Content Creation - Providers

Avatar Internet Technologies	BRA
USWeb	USA
CyberAd	USA
Desk.nt	NED
Edge Consultants Pte. Ltd.	SIN
InSite Computer Services	AUS
InterNet Korea, Inc.	KOR
Internet Publishing Group	UK
Japan Internet Communications Service	JPN
MacLand Computacion Ltda.	COL
Bluestar	JPN

TABLE 5. *Internet Landscape Matrix, (Continued)*

Redfish Group	CHI
terramedia internet service	GER
Web Hosting/Site Development	
Addlink, Inc.	USA
Aviso	DOM
BBN Planet	USA
Bulgarian Internet Company	BUL
Cognita Software Consultants	BEL
CosmodyssnAE	CAN
CyberCity (Aminet)	KOR
CyberSpace	JPN
Cylink Information Services Ltd.	CYP
Dialcom (Rent A Page)	SUI
Easynet Internet Systems	BRA
eComDE	GER
Fizgig Solutions Ltd.	UK
GES	USA
Hong Faith Enterprises Ltd.	HKG
InterPC	FRA
Internet Quality Access	NED
Internet Way	ARG
Edit & Copy	USA
HP	USA
IBM	USA
Internet Construction Company	USA
Metaphor (Meta Web)	BEL
MCI	USA
Network Technologies	AUS
NTT (Virtual Mall)	JPN
PSI	USA
SingNet (HiWay.Biz)	SIN
SuperPrism Net	CHI
UUNet	USA
Consulting & Training	
Arminco	ARM
Bluestar	JPN
Business Partners Ltd.	UK
Cambridge Technology Group	USA
China Window, Inc.	CHI
Conexus AG (LAN Service/Support)	SUI
CyberKorea	KOR
Felix & Jasper BV	NED
GIS Consulting	AUS
Great China Telecom	HKG

108

TABLE 5. *Internet Landscape Matrix, (Continued)*

Hewlett-Packard	USA
Intermarket (Internet Consulting - Firewalls, Java)	GER
MacLand Computacion Ltda.	CHI
Marben S.A./N.F.	BEL
NetConsult, AG (Networking)	SUI
Netplace Internet Consulting (WWW Services/Consulting)	GER
NetLearn	USA
NTT (Virtual Mall)	JPN
Smart S.A.	ARG
Solucions @ Web	IND
Syselog Asia	CHI
Total Peripherals Group	AUS
WebToGo	BRA
Systems Integration	
Nippon Unisys	JPN
BRAK Systems, Inc.	CAN
ChinaLink Communication & Networking	CHI
Computronics Belgium	BEL
CoreLAN Communications, Inc.	CAN
Deloitte & Touche	USA
Dendriet-Digitale Communicatie	NED
HP	USA
Siemens	USA
Intelifest Internet Marketing	UK
International Integration, Inc. (I-Cube)	USA
Migration Software Systems, Ltd.	USA
Net Effect, Inc.	USA
Netsources System Limited	HKG
Object Factory GmbH	GER
Pagework Pte. Ltd.	SIN
Cambridge Technology Partners	USA
RUCC	AUS
c-bridge	USA
ServiWEB	ARG
Systems Resources Corporation	USA
Systems Management	
Advanced Technologies Group	USA
Apertus Technology, Inc.	USA
CompuCom	USA
Decision One	USA
Digital Equipment	USA
EDS	USA
HP	USA

109

TABLE 5. *Internet Landscape Matrix, (Continued)*

InterAccess Technology Corp.	USA
JapanITS	JPN
Metrica, Inc.	USA
Pencom Systems Administration	USA
Vanstar	USA
Application Development	
Cambridge Internet Technologies	USA
Odysseus	GER
Business Re-engineering	
Anderson Consulting	USA
Index	USA
Computer Associates	USA
Business Reinvention	
Cambridge Technology Enterprises	USA
Education & Training	
Compinet Computing Centers	KOR
Heutronic (Internet-Schnupperkurs (I))	SUI
BUSINESS	
Retail	
AirLink	GER
Amazon	USA
Argentina CyberMall	ARG
Cityscape	USA
Coopertramo Net-Cabs	BRA
CUC	USA
Cyber Club Internet de Mouscron (Cyber Cafe)	BEL
Das Computerhaus (Internet Cafe)	AUT
HotSpot Internet Market	AUT
Internet Access AG	SUI
Internet Shopping Network	USA
KInterNETional	SIN
MCI	USA
Net M Communications (Aussie Internet General Store)	AUS
NRI	USA
ONSALE	USA
Réseau Internet de l'Automobile Inc.	CAN
Softline	GER
Virtual Shopping Net	SIN
Virtual Trading/Logistics	
Group Purchasing Agency	USA
industry.net	USA

TABLE 5. *Internet Landscape Matrix, (Continued)*

Financial Services	
Citicorp	USA
E-trade	USA
Cambridge Internet Fund	USA
Fidelity	USA
First Virtual Holdings	USA
Quote.com	USA
SFNB	USA
WellsFargo	USA
WorldStreet	USA
Shipping	
Federal Express	USA
UPS	USA
DHL	USA
Entertainment	
AIMC	AUS
America Online	USA
Internet Gaming Corporation	USA
Canal 33 Zap	ARG
CentralCard (Virtual City)	BRA
Cottony (Cyber Cafe)	JPN
Cyberkaffee	BEL
Cynosure	SIN
Internetcafe De Muze	NED
London Calling Internet	UK
Media Wave (Cyber Cafe)	JPN
MEDIC	JPN
NetCafe	KOR
nEthos (Cyber Cafe @ Lounge)	SUI
Shoot'n Surf	UK
Sports International	USA
TEN	USA
Worlds, Inc.	USA
News/Media	
Asahi (Asahi TV)	JPN
China Information Network	CHI
Dicas De Semana	BRA
Dow Jones	USA
First One System	HKG
Hot Wired	USA
Individual	USA
Intro AG (Intro TV)	SUI
MecklerMedia	USA

111

TABLE 5. *Internet Landscape Matrix, (Continued)*

Monthly Internet	KOR
Sarajevo OnLine	BOS
Telstra (Australian Internet Awards)	AUS
Time Warner	USA
The Times (The Times Internet Edition)	UK
Wall Street Journal	USA
Yomiuri (Shinbun)	JPN
Advertising	
Atlas Advertising	SIN
Bulgarian Internet Company	BUL
Canadiana Group	CAN
Cyber-Communications	USA
Dentsu (Total Communications)	JPN
DoubleCheck	USA
FocalLink	USA
G-Search	JPN
The Internet Agency	GER
Internet Marketing Strategy Services	CHI
CyberAd	USA
ITS	USA
Jupiter Communications	USA
Knight Ridder New Media	USA
Ogilvy & Mather	USA
Swiss Online (Swiss Online)	SUI
VM Internet Advertising & Promotions	HKG
Ziff-Davis	USA
Content Providers	
America Online	USA
Compuserve	USA
GrR Homenet (Homenet)	JPN
NetSquared Internet Solutions	UK
PointCast	USA
Pathfinder	USA
Educational Services	
Compinet Computing Centers	KOR
CyberCity	DEN
Internet Access Consultants Co.	HKG
Internet School	UK
Paideia	NED
Virtual On-Line University	USA
Business Application Components	
Cafesoft (Java Business)	USA
JLabs	AUS

TABLE 5. *Internet Landscape Matrix, (Continued)*

Velvet Palms Ltd.	UK
Health Care	
Doctor BBS	BRA
KNAW (Medical Information Centre)	NED
Financial Services	
Duine Adviesburo	NED

About The Framework

This chapter gives one framework for the Internet represented in three complimentary ways to help understand the Internet players, technology and uses:

- Figure 7-2 is the "food chain" representation for understanding the players and products.

- Figure 7-3 is the business use web representation for understanding the evolution of the software.

- Figure 7-4 is the application architectural representation for understanding the relationship among the software and hardware components in an application setting.

Figure 7-2: Internet "food chain"

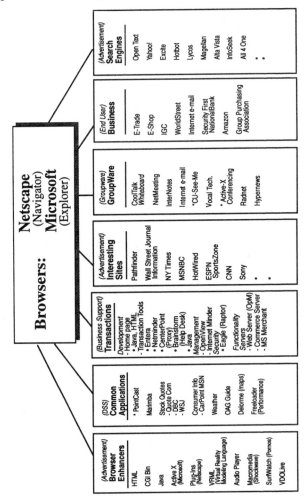

Figure 7-3: Business software tools for the Internet -
Architectural representation

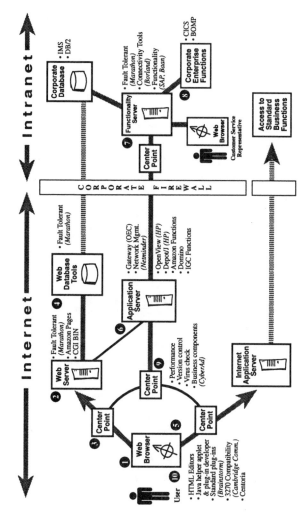

Note all three frameworks list sample products and companies. Again, these are not necessarily the best companies or the worst companies in these categories; they are merely examples.

Table 5 shows the framework for understanding the products and players in cyberspace. The first three columns list the companies and products that support business on the web. The last column outlines the end-user businesses that exist or will be created on the web and that these products support. In the first three columns, these subcategories are ordered to reflect the application architecture of Figure 7-3, starting with clients and moving through servers, management, and databases. Correspondingly, reading from left to right in Figure 7-3, you move from clients to servers to management to databases.

Food chain of the Internet

Table 5 depicts the food chain of the Internet industry. The businesses in the right columns could not exist without the businesses in the left columns. This hierarchy is an alternating series of king-serf relationships. The hardware companies are serfs to the software companies: "Please King Software Vendor, run your software on my hardware platform!" The software vendors are serfs to the service providers:

> *"Please, please, King EDS, use my software to provide your services!" Finally, the service providers are serfs to the end-user businesses:*

"Please King Bank, use my services to take your business to the web!"

The irony is that the bank is a serf to its customers such as the hardware company. Each king is a serf; each serf is a king. This is the food chain on the web.

Within each of the columns on this food chain there are subcategories. For instance, within the end-user business category there are subcategories of retail, trading, finance, and advertisement. In fact, a hierarchy similar to the one that exists among the columns exists within the columns; in the end-user category, advertising supports financial services, which, in turn, support retail.

For specifics, review Table 5 carefully. The next few sections provide an overview of some of the categories:

1. The first category, Hardware, includes hardware vendors and their products. They provide the physical devices that ensure fast, robust, and reliable networks. Their products include the machines, communications equipment, and all other physical hardware for the Internet, including the physical copper or fiber-optic lines that form the communications backbone.

2. The second category, Software, includes the vendors who provide the software tools for the creation, management, and maintainability of Internet business applications.

3. The Service providers help organizations implement business applications on the web. Some provide access. Some construct web pages and manage sites. Some aid in integrating with business processes, oth-

ers manage the entire application; and lastly some provide consulting. In addition, service providers can migrate and improve the organization's existing enterprise infrastructure and aid business processes reengineering. Their highest added value is often understanding, developing, and extending business through the correct technical solution.

4. The final category comprises the end-user businesses conducted on the web. Again, there is a hierarchy of subcategories within the end-user business category. Your business may be retail, but you would like your customers to have the ability to insure, ship, and finance orders. There are businesses today that provide and assemble these functionality components. This discussion will now provide examples that illustrate some of the categories and subcategories.

Hardware

Internet hardware comprises all the physical devices that are needed to support business transactions on the web, including computers, switches, and communication lines. The hardware can be divided into five categories:

- Clients are the devices used to browse the web, such as PCs, network computers, Java machines, and telephones. Software running on these devices makes requests to software running on server machines. In addition, Java applets, plug-ins, and other client functions are executed on these machines.

- Server machines run server applications. They contain web pages, applications, connectivity software, transaction processing, business functionality, and network management. These machines are typically more powerful than client machines. The software on the server performs the functions that the client requests such as retrieving data and computing business results such as profitability. Servers can range in price from workstations costing around $10,000 to high-end parallel processing machines costing millions of dollars.

- Database machines and legacy systems store data and handle enterprise computing. These machines typically have substantial input/output (I/O) and transaction capabilities.

- The physical network handles communication among the clients, servers, and data. This physical network of wires, fiber-optic cables, and satellites passes information between clients and servers using switches and routers. Switches and routers pass and direct traffic over the physical network. This network is called the Intranet when privately owned; it is the Internet when publicly accessible. This physical network provides the highway for information traffic.

- There exists specialized hardware devices that handle performance and security. For example, firewall devices and proxy servers check for viruses, compress data, and handle security.

Table 5 lists some of the major Internet hardware providers and their products. Some of these are described in the following sections in more detail.

Client Network Computers

These devices will be able to access the Internet without the full capabilities of the PC. The network computer will cost as little as $500. It automatically downloads all the necessary software from servers over a network. This means that, as network computer users grow in number, the systems administrator does not have to worry about client disk back-ups or data recovery; and the user can access information and applications from anywhere. Data encryption technology is in place to ensure security; and, because the software, applications, and data are stored on the server, users always get the most recent version. This will virtually eliminate the costly tasks of software acquisition, installation, administration, virus-checking, and maintenance. In a corporation, it has been estimated that the cost of maintaining a PC (virus-checking, security, version control, and administration) is $20,000 a year. With no hard drive, no floppy drive, and no supporting hardware and software, the network computer will be less expensive to maintain.

Fundamentally, because of the minimal computational capabilities of the client in this architecture, all business applications will be accessible anywhere in the world at any time from a whole new set of devices that can be plugged into phone or cable lines or through wireless access. Oracle, Samsung, and Apple have announced that they will produce these machines.

There is an ideological belief by some that these client devices will replace PCs. In this scenario, all of the office functions or run-time applets of the PC would be written in Java or another portable language, stored on web servers, and executed on an inexpensive network computer. The other view says that the downloading performance of these applets over a 9k line will be too slow and that the sophistication of the client software to run these applets too large for a network computer. They believe that the PC will live forever. What's important here is that, with a three-tiered, client/server architecture, it doesn't matter whether the PC or the network computer wins; either device can execute Internet applications on the web.

Personal Digital Assistance (PDA)

These are hand-held devices, like Hewlett Packard's Palmtop, that have been Internet-enabled. With these, you will be able to send and receive email across the Internet, as well as access news groups and retrieve other text-based information services. Companies are integrating this technology into cellular phones and pagers.

Internet Devices

There are now specialized devices that allow the combination of simultaneous Internet access and voice communication over the same phone lines such as Office 2000. That is, your home phone and Internet access lines

The Second Industrial Revolution

will look like a single line; rather than call-waiting inter-
rupting your Internet browser, a message will appear
without disconnecting the Internet session. Other Internet devices such as printers will become Internet-
enabled, hence allowing the printer to automatically
order when it is out of toner. Netscape has announced a
new company called Navio Communications to Internet-
enable TVs, phones, cars, and other consumer devices.
Office 2000 and others companies will produce these
devices.

Hardware Servers

Servers house and maintain web pages, electronic
mail, applications, connectivity, network management,
and other business functions on the Internet. Many hardware servers use Windows NT or UNIX as their operating system, but can also use legacy operating systems.
However, these operating systems have been Internet-
enabled to conform to Internet standards. Using the Java
applets and engine of c-bridge makes the operating system transparent.

There are also hardware enhancements that make
servers more suitable for use on the Internet. In a server-
centric world it is critical that the server does not fail.
One such hardware and software enhancement device is a
fault-tolerant NT extension produced by Marathon. An
enormous advantage of Marathon compared to proprietary fault-tolerant devices is that the solution requires
absolutely no changes in the existing applications.

The business implication of such a fault-tolerant machine is the maintenance of robustness for corporations with geographically disperse networks. If a natural disaster occurs in one site, all users will function without interruption. Further, mainframe and banking centers perform without ever thinking that the system is down; all date functions are automatically synchronized.

In the new world of graphics and transactions, where the servers must do huge amounts of real-time computing, performance is important. Server performance-enhancement devices include a hardware board produced by Integrated Computer Engines (ICE). This board can take a large Compaq or HP T500 (a 100 MIP machine) and turn it into a 21,000 MIP turbo-charged machine. Web servers store and maintain web pages that clients can access. A transaction server is involved in the execution and processing of business functions, whereas a web server only provides HTML and associated code. These two types of software servers can reside on the same physical server machine.

The business implication of access to a 21,000 MIP machine that costs under $300,000 is that speech and text translation, three-dimensional graphics, and complex authentication over the Internet are possible.

Communications Equipment

Communications equipment is the backbone of networks. Switches and routers are needed to support and maintain the Internet. These are hardware devices that direct traffic over the network. The market is moving from routers to switches because they are more efficient. Routers move packets of data in a serial fashion. Switches are a newer technology that increase the bandwidth on a given network segment by using multiple channels. The current cutting-edge technology in switches is the asynchronous transfer mode (ATM) which is a network protocol that allows for very high-speed data transmission.

The Internet voice standard will evolve starting with software that allows the LAN to function as a PBX. Office 2000 is developing such mechanisms. Its voice standard will further migrate to the Internet allowing robust voice over the Internet.

Modems are devices that provide the interface between computers in different locations over telephone, ISDN, and cable lines. There are a variety of modems that differ in the transmission speed. They include standard 28.8 Kb-per-second modems, ISDN modems that transfer information at a rate of 128 Kb-per-second, and cable modems with a transmission rate of 3MB per second.

There still exists today large proprietory networks; over 50% of private networks today are IBM's proprietary SNA networks. New technologies such as Cambridge Communications allow existing SNA networks to interface with the Internet TCP/IP standard.

The business benefit of the network gateway devices is that they will allow a company's substantial investment in 3270 terminals to be used for Internet access. Correspondingly such gateways will allow Internet devices to access a company's SNA network.

Internet Processors

A number of chips will support the hardware of the clients, servers, and the communications of the Internet. These chips are called Internet processors. Sun Microsystems has produced a Java chip called UltraJava that can run Java applications natively. Next-generation Internet devices will use these processors. These chips will produce high-speed inexpensive Internet devices.

Software Framework

An enormous and exponentially growing amount of software exists on the Internet. Table 5 depicts just a few. The software framework is ordered by clients, servers, and others as shown Figure 7-3.

Client Software

Software exists to create a web page, browse the web, and insert business functions into the web pages. There is also software for the server that provides security, network management, and development of specialized connectivity or functionality servers. Figure 7-2 recategorizes the software column of Table 5 with respect to the primary business use on the Internet. Table 5 shows the evolutionary use of software on the web. Conceptionaly most of the software is activated from the browser. Starting from the left of the figure are the early uses of advertising where companies would make their web site available to users throughout the world; on the right is the software to support full business transactions on the web.

Figure 7-3 gives yet another view of the software placed on a conceptual, logical architecture of application flow for the bank example used in Chapter 5. This discussion focuses on Figure 7-2.

Business Use Software Framework: Web Representation

On the top of the tree in Figure 7-2 is the browser because many web applications are activated via the browser. Within this framework business use on the Internet progresses through advertisement, decision support systems, groupware, transaction support, and end-user businesses. This discussion will now turn to specific examples of software on the Internet. Note again that this is not a complete list; only representative examples of these categories.

Web Page Tools and Capabilities

The first category of web software is devoted to advertisement. The web site has been the core of the extension of the Internet to allow for transactions. Creating a web site is the first step in the long process of reinventing your business. For example, in retail, a consumer would see an advertisement, gather information from publications such as Consumer Reports, locate a place to purchase, and arrange payment and insurance. With the advanced form of the Internet (Figure 7-2) all these functions are performed simultaneously achieving customer satisfaction and reducing the supplier cost.

This software discussion starts with an example. Figure 7-4 again depicts a picture of NationsBank's home page with information about its products, services, and branch locations. Again, this is merely an example of a web page used solely for advertisement and information gathering on the web.

Figure 7-4: NationsBank's Homepage

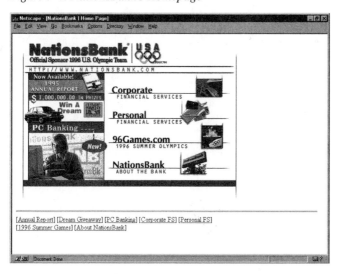

The construction of a home page such as Nations-Bank's, requires programming in the standard web language called the HTML. An HTML program is stored on a web server where a client retrieves it over the Internet using the standard protocol HTTP. The client executes the HTML program which specifies how the page should look. An HTML document includes the text to be displayed, along with links to other pages and pictures. When a browser wants to see the page, it requests a copy of the page from the web server and then displays it for the user. Until recently, creating an interesting, accurate, and effective web page was a long and tedious process.

Web Software

Software tools exist for the construction of web pages from text to rich pictures to multimedia and business transactions. Apart from describing the tools, these bullet points are important because they structure the jargon of the Internet. In short, all of these technical terms refer to technologies that improve a web page.

- HTML editors can help to quickly create the HTML programs used to create text and draw web pages.

- GIFs, JPEG, and bit maps provide formats for pictures stored on a web page

- Common Gateway Interface (CGI) tools such as Spider can call and execute remote programs from a web page. The disadvantage of using these tools for transactions are the slow performance associated with repainting the entire screen and the nonrobustness for high transaction computing.

- Tags within an HTML program allow for the insertion of applets written in Java that allow animation and interactive forms within a web page. Java tools such as J-Factor and Latté make Java code easier to write. The advantage of Java is that, since it is a cross-platform language, it can be executed on any computer or operating system.

- ActiveX (formerly OCX) builders such as Visual Basic 5 allow for Microsoft-compliant OLE objects to be placed in a web page.

- Software companies have built plug-ins that meet Netscape application program interface (API) standards. Such standard plug-ins can be placed in a web page and executed. The advantage of these standard Java applets, ActiveXs, and plug-ins is that, since they are reusable components, business applications can be inserted into any web page. The disadvantage of these is that they are bandwidth-intensive and need a specific player on the PC before they can be executed, hence requiring a big client machine.

CGI bin applets, ActiveX and plug-ins can be used to access remote databases, application servers, or legacy systems. This access from a web page is accomplished by a call from the plug-in within that page to a separate server, as depicted in Figure 7-3. These separate servers can be constructed with such tools as Web Data, Entera extension, and Microsoft ACCESS. These web tools allow for the creation of web pages that have text, pictures, animation, and business functions.

The business implication is that the web can now provide interactive dynamic pages.

Multimedia

Multimedia are some of the applications that can be provided via Java applets, ActiveX or plug-ins. The Java language has made Sun Microsystems a strong Internet player. An entire industry has been created for making web pages come alive with Java, ActiveXs, and plug-ins. Companies such as Borland and Centura have created tools that allow for easy insertion of animation into web pages. VDOLive is an example of a multimedia plug-in that allows the viewing of streamed video feeds, such as a CNN news update. Figure 7-5 shows a page using this software.

Figure 7-5: VDOLive

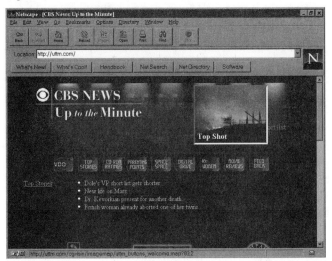

Pornography

Other supporting Internet technology includes por-
nography-checking. The ease with which pornography
can be accessed on the web has created a concern for par-
ents and corporations considering Internet usage. There
are tools such as Surf Watch that can be placed on the PC
to restrict access to pornographic web pages. Figure 7-6
depicts an attempted access to the Playboy home page.
Surf Watch looks for certain web sites or words on the
web page and allows access according to the guidelines
established by the network manager.

Figure 7-6: Result of SurfWatch pornography check

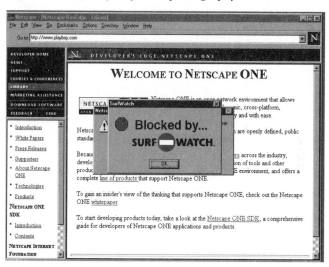

The deficiency of such programs is that they reside
on the PC. If users decide they don't want to be
restricted, they circumvent the password mechanism.

Further, these pornography checks work by scanning text tags. Today, many pornographic sites use bit maps rather than HTML. These checks are useless for preventing access to such sites. Software such as CenterPoint's pornography check, version control, and virus protection are superior because they reside on a proxy server or gateway to the Internet. Every time a client accesses the web, the transaction goes through a high-powered proxy server, then to a web server, and returns through the same route. In short, all web client traffic goes through the proxy server, allowing for uniform pornography checks, including online picture scanning, version control, and security.

Search Engines

Search engines are another category of software that supports advertising and information gathering through web pages. They allow clients to look for and obtain information accessible anywhere on the web. Search engines such as Yahoo! greatly enhanced the web by organizing the database of web sites into hierarchical categories. This organization is an advancement over search engines like InfoSeek that mainly searched for words or phrases.

Companies that supply access to search engines make money by charging companies for advertisements displayed on the home page of the search engine.

Decision Support Systems

Decision support systems (DSS) provide a capacity on the web to allow users to make informed and rapid decisions about products and stocks. Figure 7-7, shows the StockMaster site, where information exists that can be used for decisions concerning the purchase or sale of stock, including comparisons and analyses, with which more informed decisions about buying and selling securities can be made. Other sites, such as U.S. News and World Report, provide information about weather conditions and forecasts, thereby facilitating travel decisions.

Figure 7-7: StockMaster

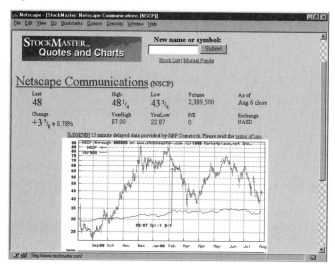

The skilled Internet user can access information about virtually any topic. This book cannot do justice to this capability on the Internet, nor to the millions of web

133

sites and applications that can be used for DSS. The best advice to the user: Browse! The best advice to corporations: Get your information on the web or else you will not even be considered in the decision!

Business implications of a web presence include:

- Companies can take advantage of all information around the world as well as their own internal information.

- Companies can make more informed decisions.

- Companies can speed up sales cycles.

- Companies can get disparate information immediately and react accordingly.

Groupware

Groupware supports the collaboration of many people, in disparate locations, on a single project. Groupware software is now emerging. Software, such as Microsoft's NetMeeting and Netscape's CoolTalk, allows a person in Hong Kong simultaneously to review and alter the same spreadsheet or document as a person in New York. Other business uses of collaborative groupware will include:

- Scheduling
- Help desk
- Customer service
- Product tracking

- Hospital records

- Prescriptions

Figure 7-8 depicts a videoconference between two business persons reviewing corporate financial statements. This conference is possible using the CU-SeeMe software package, from White Pines. The software for this can be obtained over the web at a small expense, and the camera costs about $30. Videoconferencing over the web will give unlimited long-distance phone and video for the price of Internet access fees.

Figure 7-8: CU-SeeMe

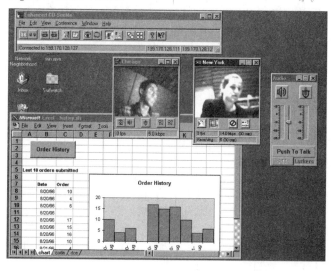

These videoconferencing capabilities are still in preliminary stages, and the emerging groupware software and networking will provide a powerful tool for global companies to conduct meetings with text, reports, and people.

Business Support Software

Figure 7-3 depicts the architectural representation of the framework. It takes a user transaction from the browser and carries it through access to customer records inside the corporation. The reader should follow ten steps in Figure 7-3:

1. Query a bank balance
2. Retrieve the web page
3. Perform compression and virus check
4. Retrieve bank static data
5. Initiate transactions
6. Activate connectivity server
7. Retrieve Intranet server
8. Access customer data
9. Secure transaction
10. Display results

Now business-support software on the Internet provides the infrastructure to support sophisticated end-user business transactions on the web as depicted in Figure 7-3. This software includes client and server development, management, transaction, legacy system access, and security. Web development tools such as Visual Basic 5 allow for the insertion into web pages of components that can directly access business servers as shown in Step 5.

On the server side, as in Steps 6 and 7 of Figure 7-3, tools exist for building connectivity, functionality and management servers. The Entera Toolkit allows server access to legacy systems. Likewise, Microsoft has tools for servers that access relational database systems such as those designed by Sybase Corporation. The functionality servers are typically written in languages such as C++ and Java.

Management tools such as Hewlett Packard's Open-View product are being enhanced to allow for the management and maintenance of Internet applications. Security tools such as Raptor's Eagle and CheckPoint build firewall software. Companies such as CenterPoint have tools for version control. Some organizations offer the basic components for doing business on the web such as shipping, financing, and insurance components. These components allow a customer to order products from one system while the business components handle the financing, shipping, and insurance.

Services

A whole industry is rapidly growing that helps customer corporations to conduct business on the web. Companies such as US Web will construct and maintain web sites. Other service providers, like c-bridge will build end-user applications on the web, including access to legacy systems and other software packages. Still other service providers manage and outsource the entire web application. Table 5 shows some of the service players. Some companies are creating seminars and workshops that will assist you in reinventing your organization, such as the CTG Reinvention Workshop.

Businesses on the Web

Table 5 depicts the end users businesses now on the web. The web is where the second industrial revolution is happening and huge industries will be created to service large end-user markets; market estimates include: $100 billion in finance, $200 billion in trading, and $400 billion in retail. These end-user Internet business industries are just starting to take off.

Returning to the oil analogy, the business associated with the drilling, processing, and distribution of oil were but a small fraction of the total business of the petrochemical industry. The Internet hardware, software, and service industries will be small compared to that of all the business and industries reinvented on the web.

Many companies already conduct business on the web. Many airlines are now selling discount tickets over the web. Similarly, Amazon.com Books, based in Seattle, has created a bookstore with all the associated processes on the web. Security First Network Bank (SFNB) is the first bank on the web.

Entertainment companies such as Ten have created software that allows multiple users to play interactive games over the web. Interactive Gaming Corporation (IGC) allows for gambling over the web. Figure 7-2 lists some of the present end-user businesses that have been reinvented around and are now running on the web.

What now exists is only a small fraction of what will be here by next year. The question is, will your business be there too?

Summary

Take your business to the web quickly, take advantage of your legacy systems, and then partner with other web businesses that have components to complete your business function; put your basic product tracking and ordering system, your basic manufacturing design system, your governmental finance and budget, or your hospital patient information out on the web, but use services for shipping and financing components to complete the business processes that you do not have.

As you read the newspapers over the next few months, place the Internet technical developments, new companies, and new applications in the matrix of Table 5, the software tree of Figure 7-2, and the architecture of Figure 7-3. If you can, this chapter has been a success.

8

Present and Future Technology

Chapter 7 discussed technologies that support reinventing your business on the web. This chapter will focus on two important technical concerns about the Internet and today's technology solutions, as well as what to expect in the future:

- Security

- Performance

Technological Summary for the Business Executive

To the business executive: Don't worry! With the resources of every major technical company, with the research of every major university and research center focused on the Internet, combined with the enormous capital of Wall Street and other financial markets, all of the technological problems of today eventually will be solved.

To the business executive who feels uncomfortable—intellectually or emotionally—with the issues of security or performance, there are alternatives that give businesses immediate advantages of the Internet without security as an issue; you can act on these now. They include:

The Second Industrial Revolution

- Use Internet standards within your organization or your private network thereby creating an Intranet that is secure from any outside threat. Your lines of communication can be augmented for the performance you need.

- Use the Internet for data access of nonsensitive information such as reporting on global product sales, order-tracking, shipping, and advertising.

- Build your Internet and Intranet applications so that they remain separate with the Internet containing no confidential information. Do not allow access through your firewall.

- Apply the same security criteria of your present systems to the Internet. For example, CTG studies indicate that you are 50 times more likely to have your credit card number stolen from a restaurant wastebasket than over the Internet; yet you still charge purchases on credit cards.

For those who still worry, read on.

Security

The most serious concern that business executives have about putting their business on the web is security. Approximately 3,000 business executives attend CTG seminars each year; when asked why they haven't taken their business to the web, an overwhelming number cite security concerns. This section will provide a framework for addressing security issues.

Figure 8-1 depicts this framework. As a client enters a transaction there are four main Internet security issues:

- Authentication of the user
- Integrity of the transaction throughout the network
- Authentication of the target web site
- Safety from intrusion into the corporate system

Figure 8-1: Security and performance framework

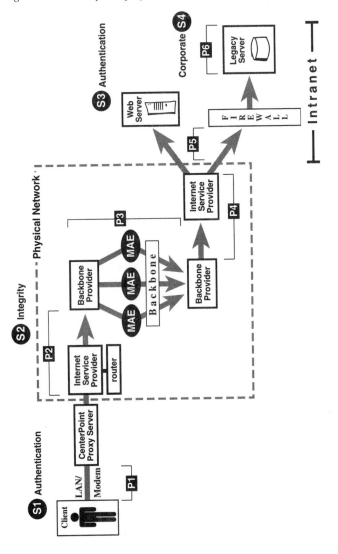

User Authentication

The first security issue is the verification of a user's identity as in S1 of Figure 8-1. Is this person who he or she claims to be? Today the most common form of identifying users is through passwords. Netscape, Microsoft, Raptor, and others all have mechanisms for implementing password identification and locking access. Companies like Verisign create a unique digital signature from a password that is recognized and accepted by content providers. In general, security tokens are passed throughout the Internet. A token, whether it is compliant with DCE, SSL, or some other standard, can be checked by all servers, allowing for limited access to each component in the enterprise. More sophisticated authentication include hardware such as Hewlett Packard's SmartCard and Security Dynamics card that can be inserted in the PC and generates a unique code that is synchronized with a server every ten seconds.

In the future, recognition of voice, retina, and fingerprints will enhance authentication. The Internet industry, where products are born and mature within eighteen months, the future does not mean five or ten years; it means that in six months to a year other methods of identity verification will appear.

Transaction Integrity

This is the security issue of S2 in Figure 8-1 where the transaction travels through the Internet. The physical network of the Internet was designed by MIT, improved by BBN, and adapted by the US military to be robust. The main objective of the military was to create a network that could withstand a nuclear attack on any switch or portion of the physical network and still function. This fault-tolerant robustness was accomplished by allowing packets of information to be dynamically routed. That is, every piece of information that travels over the Internet can take any of a number of possible routes. Furthermore, in addition to robustness, dynamic routing facilitated the growth of the Internet.

The Internet, then, is robust and can grow dramatically. So what is the problem with transaction integrity? Dynamic routing presents the possibility that the sender may never know what route that a message sent over the Internet took. An Internet highwayman (bad person) with access to an Internet node could very easily take important and confidential information from all messages that travel through its node.

How do we ensure the integrity of a message in transit? The technical solution exists. It is the encryption of all messages sent across the Internet. MIT's Kerberos security, coupled with encryption software, gives a 140-bit encryption key that provides the highest-level military Grade B security. Messages encrypted in this encryption algorithm would take centuries to break. Hence, putting Kerberos or similar software to take care of the encryption such as RSA or Digital Encryption Security (DES) standards on the client and server would ensure the integrity of all transmitted messages.

The tampering or deleting of messages is not solved with encryption.

So what is the integrity problem? US Government concerns and policies. The US Government allows financial institutions to use 140-bit encryption around the world. Current national security policy only allows the use of 140-bit encryption for message transaction within the United States for other industries. The resolution of these restrictions are complex as there is pressure to allow the global use of 140-bit encryption. Alternatively, with the rise of world terrorism governments need to be able to monitor information. Other technological alternatives will be available in the future.

The Organization for Economic Cooperation and Development (OECD) is constructing a plan for global encryption such as third-party key holders. The fundamental problem with such efforts is the necessity of achieving a worldwide consensus. Alternatively, Japan is working on its own security standards for encryption such as FEAL and the NTT triple DES trip. Encryption with smaller keys (40 bits) that will discourage all but the most sophisticated Internet thieves are now available.

Site Authentication and Alteration

Site authentication protects against an Internet wolf in sheep's clothing as shown in S3 of Figure 8-1. Basically, a bad person could steal information by constructing a site that looks like another legitimate site. Further, this person could alter your web site or steal high-priced software from your site.

The site-authentication software of Centerpoint continually validates all of the web servers accessed through its proxy server. Centerpoint registering validates the web site and a continual handshake with the web site ensures its validity.

With respect to stealing code from a web site, several software companies offer products that scramble web sites so that only authorized users can change or copy them.

Corporate Internal System Integrity

The fear here is that an Internet intruder could somehow gain access to the enterprise of a corporation as in S4 of Figure 8-1. This intruder could then access confidential information or spread computer viruses. The firewall technology of companies such as Raptor, Checkpoint, and NEC's software server ensures that authorized users have access to the corporation systems. Raptor offers further security mechanisms, such as isolating servers from general access. Traditional audit trails and mainframe security must also be used.

Performance

This section presents a framework for understanding performance issues (P1 through P6 in Figure 8-1). Anyone who has felt the frustration of accessing a home page from home with a 28.8K line knows that performance is another major concern with the Internet. The business concern is that, with poor performance, customers will not use the Internet for business transactions. Two solutions to this problem exist:

1. Increase the capacity of the pipe and switches.
2. Improve performance of the machines and software at each end to allow online compression, routing, and massive buffer memory.

Increase Bandwidth

The first issue is that of the pipe. There are six steps in business transactions over the Internet as shown in P1 through P6 of Figure 8-1.

The first (P1) is from the client to the Internet service provider. Slow modems will be replaced by cable modems, ISDN modems, or Hewlett Packard's super modems. The physical connection varies widely depending on your location; most homes in Holland have ISDN lines whereas few in Brazil have even 9k lines.

The second (P2) is from the Internet service provider to the backbone provider. This starts from a modem rack or an ethernet network then to a router and then through a high-speed line. The problem here is that there is little redundancy; that is, if the network or router fails, your Internet connection goes down.

The third (P3) is from backbone provider to backbone provider including MCI, BBN, and Sprint. The biggest problem here is the vulnerability of the metropolitan area exchanges (MAEs) that dynamically direct traffic.

The Second Industrial Revolution

Think of six million roads converging in a few intersections each with a single police officer madly directly traffic. The company that runs all MAEs is MFS Communications, recently purchased by Worldcom. Another problem here is with the routers. The routers must constantly know what lines are up and down. The size of the routing maps has been increasing faster that the memory technology capacity within the routers.

The fourth (P4) is the inverse transaction of P2 and has the same performance vulnerability, namely lack of redundancy. The fifth (P5) is the inverse transaction of P1 without the modem and has the same vulnerability; that is, the communication lines to the backbone provider.

The sixth (P6), the web site itself, might not have the software capable of handling the volume nor the web site itself may not have fault-tolerant machines or software.

The solution to the Internet capacity and performance problem is not a one-step process; as the Internet grows so will the capacity problems. By analogy, as the use of electricity grew in the US, so did the problems with the electrical power grid. Each decade, as the grid grew larger, new capacity issues surfaced and were solved. For example, in 1965 the electric power grid failed causing a domino effect of blackouts from Boston to New York. Nine months later there was an unusual increase in the US population. There was a severe collapse of the electrical power grid and then solutions were found. We still have electricity on the East Coast.

Some solutions to these Internet capacity and performance problems include:

- charging for guaranteed performance

- the development of better routers by companies such as CISCO

- the installation of ATM networks that can handle significantly more traffic by companies like MFS allowing group addresses to be clumped together; that is, class list, inner domain routing (CIDR)

In general, with respect to network performance problems and site performance problems, the efforts for solutions are journeys not destinations, as each solution encourages more users. The good news is the opportunity for solutions providers; there are many organizations working on these issues

Improve Performance Over Slow Lines

An alternative to increasing the capacity or speed of the lines is the use of high-speed, large-memory proxy servers and sophisticated client machines. The proxy server is connected to the web server with a high speed line (a T1 or T3 carrier.) The client connection to the proxy server (P1 of Figure 8-1), however, may be a slow line; for example, 28.8K. All client requests for information or transactions on a server will first go to the proxy server. The proxy server then retrieves and returns the information to the client. Its compression techniques take images and converts them to wavelets, at a 100/1 compression rate. It makes 100 bits of information look like 1 bit for Internet travel. The compressed information is then sent to the client where it is decompressed. Compressing proxy servers with the appropriate compression software can give a 28.8K line the performance of an ISDN line.

To support the speed required to make compression in real time, Centerpoint uses a high-speed parallel processing board made by ICE. The ICE board provides a supercharge to machines to make them act like 21,000 MIP machines.

In the future, such proxy servers supported by massively parallel processors will be commonly distributed throughout the Internet.

Summary

In short, these are difficult problems that are being worked on by many people. Today, however, solutions exist that allow for satisfactory security and performance for most of your applications.

Part 4

Managing the Change

Destroy the Impediments

I have stated that this book is about business strategies and the Internet; however, it is really about change!

Reinvention of your company will result in a drastic set of changes including:

- Different company organization

- Different employee job functions

- Different customers.

Moving your business transactions to the Internet also requires additional changes including:

- Your relationship with distributors

- New technologies for your IT department

Will anyone in your organization resist these changes? Yes! Almost everyone will. What will your biggest obstacle be when reinventing your business infrastructure? Changing people! How do you overcome obstacles of changing people in your organization?

This nontechnical, nonbusiness discussion about changing people may seem most unusual for a business-on-the-Internet book. On a personal note, most CEOs who come to Cambridge Technology Group seminars, rate management of change as a top concern. This is a brief guide to the most complex subject: How you can manage the change of your people to a new business and the Internet environment?

A fundamental concept with trying to change people is that humans are the most adaptable species on earth. People change all the time. You behave one way with your spouse, and the very next second a different way with a taxi driver. The question is: What impediment is preventing a person from changing?

Table 6 lists ten impediments to change in the left column. The right column briefly states the action needed to remove the impediment. Each of the impediments is discussed subsequently in more detail. This matrix and discussion are a road map for how to eliminate the barriers to change in your journey to the reinvention of business and the incorporation of the Internet.

TABLE 6. *Road Map to removing impediments to change*

Impediments to Change	Your Action
1. Lack of vision	Listen to customers; formulate
2. Lack of shared and correct vision	Provide structure, understand, losses, disseminate
3. Lack of judgement	Reality-test, analyze, act

TABLE 6. *Road Map to removing impediments to change, (Continued)*

Impediments to Change	Your Action
4. Defensiveness	Focus on organization: • Agreed goals • Agreed CSF • Resolution
5. Old ways of thinking	Educate
6. Culture	Make explicit your culture
7. Success	Maintain vigilance
8. Lack of trust	Use your trust or ambassador; keep trust with honesty
9. Not using power/ authority	Use your power
10. Crabs	Identify cynics and contain or fire them

Table 6 may be the most important page in this book; Change is everywhere and the need to lead and manage it is critical.

1. Lack of a Vision

If you don't have a vision, other people will not change for you; they will not follow you; and they will not find you inspiring. If you do not have a vision for yourself, personally, you will not know what road you should take. On the road to successful business reinvention, the lack of vision is an impenetrable brick wall. It not only impedes progress, but it also allows no light to fall on the road ahead. Without a vision you and your team will inevitably end up in a ditch.

Listen to Customers: Formulate

How do you acquire a new vision for your company in the Internet? There are many ways: having an inspirational mentor, conducting retreats with your senior management, attending executive seminars, listening to your customers, and reading books like this.

CSN, WP&L, and O.C. Tanner Awards all crystallized their vision of reinventing their firms and using the Internet via executive seminars at CTG. As another example, 30 years ago, Ross Perot founded a small consulting firm, EDS. Mort Meyerson was hired shortly after to be president. Meyerson's first task was to poll customers. He learned of their need and formulated the vision of facilities management. As a result, he and Perot built a $4 billion company on that vision.

For your business vision, listen to customers, trust your advisors, and your intuition; and formulate your strategy from those discussed earlier. For your personal vision, dream. Then proceed to overcome the next obstacle: lack of shared vision.

2. Lack of Shared and Correct Vision

The next roadblock will be your ability to share your vision with people responsible for implementation. How do you share your vision of using the Internet for business? What are the brick walls stopping others from seeing and accepting your vision? How do you blow them up? Your ability to share your vision with your colleagues rests on your ability to give structure to the new vision. You must carefully recognize the losses entailed with the destruction of their old structure and address and replace those losses.

For example, people dug up old bones for thousands of years. It wasn't until Charles Darwin created the structure of the theory of evolution that people could see the continuity of millions of years of animal evolution and recognize these bones as dinosaurs. However, with that new evolutionary structure, many old structures, such as those upheld by religious groups, crumbled. With any change, there will be gains and losses. Sell your shared vision. However, don't forget to consider the losses that your people will sustain; for example, the 20-year veteran COBOL programmer's loss of self-esteem.

How did James Morgan, president of Shell Oil, express his vision of a reinvented Shell America? He conducted an executive seminar for his senior management. He was able to share his vision effectively by showing his executives a pilot Internet application that achieved their business goals.

Provide Structure, Understand Losses, Disseminate

Adding structure to vision may come in the form of company meetings, similar to those that Bill Gates of Microsoft held to reinvent his company around the Internet. To add structure to the introduction of new Internet technologies, implementing pilot Internet projects for all to see has proven successful. Paul O'Neill, CEO of ALCOA, added structure to his vision that IT could help business by assigning six people to build a global order-entry system in twelve weeks. He then authorized CTG and the six developers to demonstrate the power of this new vision of technology to 700 of his technical people. ALCOA is now well on the road to transforming its business and IT strategies. This same method of adding structure by sharing a vision of the power of Internet-driven IT was employed by Mike Goldberg, former CFO of Mobil Oil Corp.; the John Deere Company; Gen. Alonzo Short of the US Defense Information Systems Agency; and by Wisconsin Power & Light to give structure to an Internet vision. All of these executives used pilots and were successful at adding structure in order to implement a shared vision of new Internet and IT technology.

3. Lack of Judgment

In order to choose the correct road, correct business strategy, and correspondingly the right vision, you need good judgment. Virtually everything you do professionally and personally requires it.

Should I get on the Internet? Am I ready? Is it ready? These are just a few judgment questions. There are three road blocks to good judgment:

- Poor reality testing
- Poor analysis
- Poor action

You must blow up each of these brick walls with your skepticism, objectivity, and decisiveness. When making a judgment, the following three actions must be taken:

Reality Testing

You can't make a judgment until you have facts; meanwhile, retain a healthy skepticism. You need to gather the relevant data, be skeptical, and seek help from people who will tell you the truth. Your fail-safe tactic is having people around who will tell you the truth. In an extreme case, you need someone to tell you that the emperor has no clothes. Unfortunately, there are very few people who will tell you the truth, and very few people from whom you will accept it.

With respect to the Internet, talk to users and businesses that are early adopters. Encourage your people to help you with reality testing for each of your judgments.

Analyze

In school, we were constantly given data and trained to analyze it. However, to analyze data correctly, we must remain unbiased and neutral. These are the same analytic and reasoning tools that you learned in mathematics, philosophy, and other courses. But don't overanalyze problems and get stuck in analysis paralysis. Especially with respect to the Internet, speed is as important as accuracy!

Act

Lack of action can halt your business growth. Another brick wall now looms in front of you. The plastic explosive that can totally obliterate this wall is your own decisiveness! Being decisive is just the opposite of being unbiased; it's on the opposite end of the spectrum from being skeptical. In this mode you must act. You must have the passion to convey the importance of your actions to your people

Consider making the judgment of adapting to the business reinvention strategies and Internet infrastructure set forth in this book. If you find yourself saying "I'll wait a little longer before moving to the Internet," where is the passion ? Get help from someone who will shout: "YOU MUST ACT NOW!"

You cannot wait to start reinventing you organization or getting on the Internet. If you do, your company will die.

4. Defensiveness

Another brick wall along the road to business success will be the defensiveness of your people; those who want to retain the old ways with which they are familiar. The person who developed the old product under the old methodology will be the last to let it go; certainly the last to suggest the reinvention the corporation. We all know of the founders of great companies who had to be removed because they defended the old product and old company that they built. Over time, some of those prod-

162

ucts became obsolete, and the companies had to move on. Similarly, family members defend positions that are no longer good for them or the rest of the family. You too may be silently defending some adapted characteristic that is keeping you from achieving your dream.

The adaptation of the Internet will elicit defensiveness, not only from your technical people. What is your sales department going to say about the loss of commission with orders over the Internet? How about your distributors? They will all be defensive! With respect to reinventing your corporation, what will all your departments say? No, no, no!

Focus on the Organization

The weapon you can use to blow up defensiveness is a process that lays a series of explosive traps. The idea is to get the people who are defensive to agree on a set of goals for your organization and what is critical to meeting these goals. Next, get those who are defensive and any others to examine the position they are defending within the context of the agreed-upon goals and critical success factors. In the face of this process, incorrect defensive positions often crumble.

For example, the old guard at Hemersley Iron, an Australian company that produces 12% of the world's iron ore, defended the old way of doing business. In a week-long process, the chairman got the key management and the old guard together and they jointly developed and agreed on these goals for the company. These goals were placed on their business cards:

Hemersley is the company that:

- Everyone wants to work for

- Everyone wants to own

- Everyone wants to do business with

The critical success factors to which Hemersley management group then agreed included a new emphasis on employee satisfaction, stockholder return, and customer focus. The old way of doing business was then addressed. The defenders' outmoded ideological stance was shed like a lobster sheds its shell so that it can grow. The company was then reinvented.

5. Old Ways of Thinking

If your people are unfamiliar with new ideas, the obstacle is their own thought process. The way to blow up this obstacle is through education. CTG surveys indicate that there is a huge lack of people trained in Internet technology and use. The old way of thinking for technical people is COBOL, CASE, and other methodologies; not Java, web, and HTML.

Educate

Senior management must launch a massive educational program not only in the new technologies, but also in business. How many of your technical people know the difference between the business measures of return on assets and return on investments? Do they know why one of these numbers for a bank may be 10% while another may be 2%? It is important to understand both the business and technical sides of the corporation because, in the new reinvented company, the technologies of the Internet are closely woven into business strategies.

In order to overcome their old ways of thinking, your customers, your people, and your government need to be educated with your new vision, new products, and services. For example, James Duckworth, the CIO at Unilever, needed to change the entire management from its old way of seeing IT as a cost center to the new view of IT as a benefit center. Unilever brought all of their top management to Cambridge, Mass., USA, for a CTG seminar on how IT could help its business. A survey taken before the seminar indicated that, on average, executives rated IT very low as a strategic weapon for business. At the end of the seminar, the opinion of IT rose 300%. Lack of understanding was overcome with education.

6. Culture

Another brick wall in the road to change is the culture of your people and your culture. Technical people tend to be averse to risk. Sales people promote a culture of aggressiveness. Japanese culture promotes respect for authority. European culture tends to be structured. Americans tend to be spontaneous. There are two main issues:

1. How do you prevent your culture from getting in the way?

2. How do you change someone else's culture?

Make Explicit Your Culture

With respect to your culture, be careful to recognize the diverse cultures of others. They may misinterpret your efforts, because, in their culture, your actions could have a different meanings. For example, your enthusiasm to a European group may be viewed with suspicion whereas a US group expects it. Japanese executives are more uncomfortable in a classroom setting where they may present a wrong answer, whereas a Harvard Business School culture encourages such settings. The Internet is global. Your use of the Internet for your business will place your organization right up against these cultural issues, so be aware of and sensitive to them. Make your culture meanings explicit to the people you are trying to change.

Changing Culture

If your business strategy requires risk, how do you overcome the cultural impediment to risk that people have? A tool you can use is to put people into a group that has the culture you want them to have. For example, NEC regularly sends its people to other countries to experience their manufacturing cultures.

Another method of changing people's culture is through the introduction of structured guidelines. You can of course impose a new culture. In 1965, when Singapore became a separate country from Malaysia, some thought Singapore was doomed. Today, with 3 million people, it is the No. 2 oil-refining nation in the world and No. 4 in trading. This disciplined, hardworking culture was created, structured, and strictly enforced by its leader, Lee Kuan Yew.

Your technical people may feel uncomfortable with the unstructured culture of the Internet. If they are put together with recent college graduates or in a student Internet development environment, they too may adapt to this culture.

7. Success

We have all heard that if it isn't broken, don't fix it! Present success is precisely the brick wall that may be the impediment to your future success. Of the Fortune 500 companies in 1950, 50% no longer exist. Why?

Why wouldn't you reinvent you company now? You may say that it is successful the way it is. Watch out! Why wouldn't you move to the Internet? You may say that you are doing just fine without new technology. Watch out!

Why didn't IBM, who dominated the computer market, move into client/server and open systems technology sooner? Why didn't Digital move more aggressively into UNIX, a technology that it helped to develop? Both of these companies had enormous success with current products. The implicit argument from executives of IBM and Digital was: "We are earning enormous profits, therefore, we are successful. Why change?"

Maintain Vigilance

The weapon that will blow up the barrier of success is constant vigilance. You must develop and institutionalize metrics. You must put methods in place to gather data on those metrics for all aspects of your organization, including customer and employee feedback.

John Young, retired chairman and CEO of Hewlett Packard Corp., brought that company from $3 billion to $16 billion in annual revenue. He used vigilance to overcome the implement of success. At the height of his success, he gave each sales person a watch to monitor and measure metrics. It had an alarm that went off every 45 minutes. He instructed the salespeople to write down what they were doing each time it went off. He found out that 75% of the time the salespeople were correcting errors in orders or reconfiguring systems. He immediately instituted a project to reengineer the entire order-fulfillment process. Note that his vigilance in examining Hewlett Packard's process resulted in increasing profits; although, initially, nothing appeared to be wrong.

The Internet is a wonderful vehicle for constantly monitoring your customer acceptance and opinions about your products. Imagine how your business will grow with a connection to 50 million customers or potential customers worldwide!

8. Lack of Trust

If people don't trust you, they will not change for you. This brick wall is rooted in suspicion, deceit, and misunderstandings. It can be blown up by honesty or a trusted emissary. Simply tell the truth. If you have made a mistake, admit it.

You may consider having third-party trusted ambassadors who can explain the implication of the Internet to skeptical employees. For example, skeptical employees will often be more easily convinced by a third party than someone internal that they may feel has a hidden agenda.

9. Not using Power and Authority

Power and authority are two weapons you can use to change people.

- Power is something you have. It's your conviction, your passion, your energy, and your knowledge. The more you use it, the more of it you get.

- Authority is something that is given to you. It is your title; your position. The more you use it, the more you lose it.

For example, a professor may use his title and his position of authority to try to make you adopt Internet technology. You will probably ignore the professor. However, if that same person offers to work with you on a pilot Internet project, he is using the power of his commitment to help you understand and embrace the new technology. You will probably participate and change.

If you use authority to change someone when you should have used power, then you will fail. The same thing will happen if you use power when authority was appropriate.

10. Crabs

On a personal note, I developed the following analogy from a fishing experience with my daughter. We took our small boat out in the summer to catch lobsters and crabs. One day I suggested to Maureen, as she placed the crabs in the basket, that we needed to put a cover over the basket so the crabs wouldn't crawl out and return to their ocean home. She said, "No, Dad, watch what happens. When one starts to crawl out, the others reach up and pull the crab back down."

If you are going to change your people, you must neutralize and destroy the crabs within your organization. There are the employees who will grab the people you want to change and pull them back into the old ways of doing business.

How can you identify a crab? Crabs move only sideways or backwards. Crabs can only tell you what won't work; but will not give an alternative. Crabs are cynics; that is, people who have given up but are still talking!

What is going to happen when you introduce these new business and Internet strategies in your organization? Some will say: "This will never work. Nothing ever works. We will not change." Your radar should go off, "Crab alert !"

Crabs are different than skeptics. Skeptics will doubt, but they will explore alternatives; and, once they believe, they will change to follow you. Crabs destroy visions!

Identify Cynics and Contain them

What weapon do you use to neutralize crabs? Boil them! Contain them. If possible, dismiss them from your organization. They are a cancer. They will destroy your vision, your leadership, and your company.

Other Impediments

The list in Table 6 is not exhaustive; other barriers to change include lack of support structure, lack of leadership, lack of self-esteem, fear, and envy. We have discussed some of the major impediments; all require your examination and careful, decisive action.

Summary

These are the impediments. Use the weapons discussed here to blow up all the brick walls along your continuing journey to success so that your people will change to implement your vision of business on the Internet.

10

Call to Action

As Chairman Lee of Samsung said: "When you take the first step on a journey, you are half-way there." The Internet revolution compels you to take two steps, one in business and one in technology, on your journey to business on the web. You must dream of where you want your business to be in the future and see that dream implemented on the Internet.

Looking back through this book, we have discussed ways for you to develop new business and technology strategies, reinvent your company, and change your people. All of this information boils down to one thing. As a business person, you must not only have dreams but the passion and will to implement them.

With respect to implementing this dream, business on the Internet will require you to find technological partners you can trust; someone who will help you through the maze of self-seeking, inappropriate, wonderful, and terrible technological solutions in this new field.

The basic premise of this book is that, if you don't take your business to the Internet, your business will be severely handicapped in the future and will eventually die. If this premise is true, then you must get started immediately. As this book has suggested, you can start with technology, building your web site and even your business on the Internet. Or you can develop your business vision and turn the technology over to a trusted technological partner and have that partner get you on the Internet. Whatever route you choose, get started and get started now! The future…is today!

Notes

The Second Industrial Revolution

Notes

The Second Industrial Revolution

Notes

The Second Industrial Revolution

Notes

The Second Industrial Revolution

Notes

The Second Industrial Revolution

Glossary

.com, .edu - These are the standard classifications of an Internet site. Companies get a designation of *.com*, schools and educational facilities get *.edu*, and military agencies are *.mil*. Others are: Government *.gov*, Internet users with no affiliation *.net*. Institutions originating in foreign countries are also differentiated: Japan *.jp*, Germany *.de*, Switzerland *.ch*, and United Kingdom *.uk*.

3270 Screen - Character-based IBM display terminal used for mainframes and minicomputers. Usually green text on a black background—the green screen.

56k Line - A digital phone line connection, or leased line, capable of carrying 56,000 bits per second. At this speed, a megabyte of data would take about 3 minutes to transfer.

ActiveX - Microsoft's standard for plug and play OLE plug-in components over the Internet.

Adobe Acrobat - Adobe Systems' software for creating documents that are viewable and printable on any platform.

AIX - IBM's implementation of UNIX.

ALPHA - Digital's new, high-performance computing architecture.

API - Application Programming Interface. This list of functions defines how to access a product.

The Second Industrial Revolution

Applet - The name for the class of applications being designed and developed for the Internet. They are called "applets" because they are not full applications, but merely pieces of a larger application. Application modules used within web pages developed in Java, ActiveX, or as plug-ins.

ARPANet - Advanced Research Projects Administration Network. The precursor to the Internet. Developed in the late 1960's and early 1970's by the U.S. Department of Defense as an experiment in wide-area networking that could survive a nuclear war.

AS/400 - Application System 400 an IBM midrange computer.

ATM - Asynchronous transfer mode (ATM) is an international high-speed, high-volume, packet-switching transmission protocol standard. ATM currently accommodates transmission speeds from 64 Kbps to 622 Mbps.

Baan - A Dutch company that produces a software packets that integrates manufacturing, finance, ordering, and human resources. Its latest release (Baan IV) was designed with a client/server architecture.

Backbone - A high-speed line or series of connections that forms a major pathway over a network.

Bandwidth - Terminology used to indicate the transmission or processing capacity of a system or of a specific location in a system (usually a network system).

Baud - Bits At Unit Density. A unit of transmission speed equal to the number of times the state (or condition) of a line changes per second. The baud rate usually refers to the number of bits transmitted each second.

BBN - Internet access provider. This company and many like it provide corporations with access to the Internet.

Bits - A binary digit; either a 0 or 1. The smallest element of a computer program. In the US, 8 bits equal one byte.

BPS - Bits-Per-Second - A measurement of how fast data moves from one place to another. A 28.8k modem can move 28,800 bits per second.

Browser - Software programs that retrieve, display, and print HTML documents from the World Wide Web. [See HTML.]

Byte - The fundamental unit that a computer uses in its operation. It is a group of adjacent binary digits, usually 8, often used to represent a single character.

C++ - Most commonly used object-oriented programming language. Built upon the language C, C++ has extensions for classes, support for inheritance, polymorphism, and encapsulation.

Caching - Storing or buffering data in a temporary location so that the information can be retrieved quickly by an application.

CAD - Computer-Aided Design. This class of software is used primarily by engineers. CAD software exists for design, testing, and modeling; and for many industries including, airline, automotive, computer chip, and most other manufacturing industries.

CASE - Computer-Aided Software Engineering. This is a class of software that allows developers to design and build software applications more easily. There are two classes of CASE tools, Upper Case and Lower Case. The Upper Case tools are design and logical flow chart generators. Lower Case tools generally generate skeleton code and pseudocode.

CGI - Common Gateway Interface: It is a convention between HTTP server implementers about how to integrate gateway scripts and programs written in any one of many popular languages: C, C++, Perl, TCL, or as shell scripts. [See HTTP.]

CICS - Customer Information Control System. An IBM transaction system that interfaces between terminal users and host applications.

CISC - Complex Instruction Set Computing. An older hardware architecture, as opposed to RISC.

Client - A program that requests services from other programs (servers) which may or may not be located on the same physical machine.

Client/Server - A paradigm of application architecture which stresses modularity and componentizing. Three-tiered client/server applications are broken into their main parts: presentation, functionality, and data. It is now the prevailing application design paradigm. Two-tiered client/server applications only break the application into two distinct parts; either presentation/functionality and data, or presentation and functionality/data.

COBOL - Common Business-Oriented Language. This language is used extensively on mainframes and mini-computers. It was designed for business applications in a centralized computing environment; however, newer releases include graphical interfaces and a more modularized software architecture.

Cookie - The cookie is information that the HTTP request carries about the user, the user's machine, and the resultant page. This information is not usually displayed on the web page or anywhere else; it is accessible through a programmers interface.

Compression - A technique for taking an image, text, audio, or any other medium, and representing it with fewer bits. This is used to speed up Internet transfer times for images and video for downloading or remote viewing. Compressing an object implies that a decompression will occur at the destination back into its original form, or a close facsimile.

CORBA - Common Object Request Broker Architecture. An object-oriented standard for distributed applications.

DBMS - Database Management System. Software that creates and manipulates data on behalf of external users or programs (e.g., IMS, HP's Image).

DCE - Distributed Computing Environment. An RPC-based standard for distributed applications defined by the Open Software Foundation.

DES - Data Encryption Standard. A cryptographic algorithm for the protection of unclassified computer data. This is not approved for national security or classified documents. This algorithm is not exportable from the US.

DME - Distributed Management Environment. A set of services for managing applications in DCE.

Domain Name - The unique name that identifies an Internet site (e.g., *ctgroup.com*). A domain name always has two or more parts, separated by periods. The part to the left of the period is the most specific, and the part on the right is the most general.

DOMF - Distributed Object Management Framework. An object-oriented standard for distributed applications.

DOS - Disk Operating System. An operating system for PCs.

DSOM - Distributed System Object Model. A multi-platform version of SOM that supports the CORBA standard.

EC - Electronic Commerce. Business environment integrating electronic transfer and automated business systems.

EDI - Electronic Data Interchange. Computer-to-computer exchange of structured transactional information between autonomous computers.

Email - Electronic mail. Messages, usually text, sent from one person to another via computer. Email can be sent automatically to a large number of addresses.

Encina - OLTP services by Transarc for DCE.

Encryption - A process of converting plain text to equivalent cipher text by means of a code or to append redundant check symbols to a message for the purpose of generating an error-detection and correction code. A method to secure and ensure documents, passwords, or information integrity between intended parties.

Ethernet - A very common method of networking computers in a LAN. Ethernet will handle about 10,000,000 bits per second and can be used with almost any kind of computer.

Fault Tolerance - The extent to which a functional unit will continue to operate at a defined performance level even though one or more of its components are malfunctioning.

Firewall - This combination of software and hardware will allow only authorized access to functionality on the other side of the firewall.

Gateway - A hardware or software mechanism that translates between two dissimilar protocols. Any mechanism for providing access to another system's functionality or data.

GIF - Graphics Interchange Format. This is a file type used to designate compressed images of a standard format.

Glass-Stiegel Act - A law which limits banks from trading and traders from banking.

Gopher - An Internet protocol that directly preceded the WWW, created by the University of Minnesota. It is a more basic system than the Web's HTTP.

GUI - Graphical User Interface. A user presentation that allows for text and graphics.

Home Page - The first HTML (Hypertext Markup Language) page that users generally see on a World Wide Web site. The home page represents the image that a company or individual projects to users on the Internet. [See HTML.]

Hot Java - A new generation of browser technology developed by Sun Microsystems which allows users to observe and interact with Java programs.

HP9000 - A class of Hewlett-Packard UNIX machines.

HP/UX - Hewlett-Packard's implementation of UNIX.

HTML - HyperText Markup Language. A simple coding system used to format documents for viewing by World Wide Web clients. HTML can be compared with early word-processing software, in which all special type, like bold or underline, need to be marked or tagged to let the printer know that the character requires special consideration during output.

HTTP - HyperText Transfer Protocol. An Internet computer communication-encoding standard for the exchange of documents on the web.

HTTPS - HyperText Transfer Protocol Secure. In the World Wide Web, a protocol that facilitates the transfer of hypertext-based files between local and remote systems using the SSL security protocol.

Hyperlink - The path between two documents that allows the user to point-and-click on specific words on the screen and thereby move to the requested location, wherever it is on the Internet.

Hypertext - Generally, any text that contains "links" to other documents; words, graphics, or phrases in an online document that can be chosen by a reader and cause another document to be retrieved and displayed.

IDL - Interface Definition Language. A high-level language in which a developer defines how programs interact with each other.

IMAP - Internet Message Access Protocol. This is another internet mail system. The IMAP message system is a client/server application replacing mainframe messaging systems.

IMS - Information Management System. An IBM database management system that runs on mainframes and internally stores information in a hierarchical model.

Internet - The term for the network of machines around the world connected via TCP/IP. The Internet consists of standards for communications and software applications.

Internet Explorer - Microsoft's Internet browser with image, text, sound, and other document-type support. The newest release contains support for ActiveX.

Intranet - A private network that uses the same software standards as the Internet but with the addition of hardware and software to limit access to or from external sources.

IPX - Internet Packet Exchange. A low-level networking protocol used by Novell to run its popular networking software.

ISDN - Integrated Services Digital Network - A digital telephonic system made up of two 64 Kbps B channels for data and one 16 Kbps D channel for management.

ISO - International Standards Organization. A standards committee based in Europe.

ISP - Internet Service Provider. A business that allows companies and individuals to connect to the Internet by providing the interface to the Internet backbone.

Java - Language developed by Sun Microsystems. This language is similar to C++. Used primarily for Internet application development. Java is used to create applets for web pages and standalone Internet applications. It is the development language and environment for the Internet.

JPEG - Joint Photographic Experts Group. Compression algorithm for still full-color or gray-scale digital images of "natural", real-world scenes.

Kerberos - A security mechanism that is compliant with the highest US Military Grade B standard. Kerberos was developed at MIT and incorporated into DCE.

LAN - Local Area Network. Decentralized cluster of interconnected computers.

Leased Lines - A permanent physical connection between two locations that forms a private wide-area network (WAN). They are called leased lines because they are rented from a telephone company.

The Second Industrial Revolution

Legacy System - Usually the name given to systems which have been in operation for many years. These machines are usually mainframes or minis, utilized in a centralized computing environment.

LU6.2 - Logical Unit 6.2. A protocol within SNA defining how two computer programs can talk to each other.

Middleware - The class of application ware or software that provides functionality or connectivity in the second tier of the three-tiered architecture, between the presentation and the data.

MIME - Multipurpose Internet Mail Extensions. The standard for how to send multipart, multimedia, and binary data using the world-wide Internet email system, e.g. images, audio, wordprocessing documents, programs, or even plain text files.

MIPS - Million Instructions per Second. A processor performance benchmark.

Modems - Modulator/Demodulator. Hardware communication devices used to interface digital computers and terminals to analog, phone, ISDN, and cable lines. SLIP (serial line Internet protocol) is software used in conjunction with a modem to emulate TCP/IP. Using SLIP will allow a remote machine to access file servers, application servers, the Internet, or mail servers.

Mosaic - User interface software for navigating, browsing, and accessing files on the Internet. The Mosaic browser was developed at NCSA, the National Center for Supercomputing Applications at the University of Illinois.

Motif - A GUI standard defined by OSF.

MPEG - Moving Picture Experts Group. A proposed International Standard Organization (ISO) standard for digital video and audio compression for moving images. The primary application targeted during the MPEG-2 definition process was the all-digital transmission of broadcast-quality video.

MVS - The operating system for IBM mainframes, recently updated to MVS Open Edition. This adds support for DCE and a client/server architecture while still maintaining a centralized mainframe architecture

Naming Service - Service in a distributed environment that provides a client program with the location of the server programs it needs.

NCP - Network Control Program. A program that manages the top of an SNA domain, usually on a mainframe.

NCS - An RPC-based standard for distributed applications defined by HP and used as a base for the RPC mechanism used by DCE.

Netscape - Company whose browser, Netscape Navigator, has driven the popularity of the World Wide Web. The browser is able to display images, text, and, with the assistance of plug-ins and helper apps, audio, video, 3-D images, virtual reality, and many other document types.

NetMinder - JETS' network management service for distributed applications.

NFS - Network File System. Allows the users of one computer to use the disk of another computer as if it were part of their local machine.

ODE - Open Distributed Environment. An environment for high-level implementation of distributed applications; compliant with major distributed technology standards, including OSF, DCE, and UI ATLAS.

OLAP - On-line Analytic Processing. A set of programs and methodologies that provide the framework necessary for real-time analysis and calculation.

OLE - Object Linking and Embedding. This is an industry standard set forth by Mcirosoft for object oriented computing and communications.

OpenVMS - A version of VMS that complies with open systems software.

OS - Operating System. The software that controls a computer's devices.

OS/2 - IBM's graphical operating system for PCs.

OSF - Open Software Foundation. A consortium of vendors developing standards for open systems; sponsored by IBM, Digital, HP, and others.

OSI - Open Systems Interconnect. A networking model proposed by ISO; its layered structure allows interoperability of networking protocols.

PBX - Private Branch Exchange - A subscriber-owned telecommunications exchange that usually includes access to the public switched network. A private telephone switchboard that provides on-premises dial service and may provide connections to local and trunked communications networks.

PeopleSoft - PeopleSoft is best known for its Human Resources application, but have recently shipped both a Financial and Manufacturing module.

PGP - Pretty Good Privacy. This is a method of data-encryption that allows people to communicate securely on the Internet.

Plug-Ins - Software programs that extend the capabilities of Netscape Navigator in a specific way. Plug-ins will, for example, extend Navigator to be able to play streamed audio or video, or read virtual reality or multimedia documents. Macromedia's Shockwave, Summus' Wavelet, and Progressive Networks' RealAudio are a few examples plug-ins.

POP - Internet Access - Point of Presence. A term used by Internet service providers to indicate the number or geographical locations of their access to the Internet.

POP3 - Post Office Protocol 3. This is a standard protocol used for Internet mail systems, used by many Internet mail applications.

POSIX - API standards defined by the Institute of Electrical and Electronic Engineers (IEEE) to guarantee that a program will be portable from one operating system to the other.

PPP - Point-to-Point Protocol. Best known as a protocol that allows a computer to use a regular telephone line and a modem to make a TCP/IP connection, and thus be on the Internet. PPP is gradually replacing SLIP for this purpose.

Public Key Cryptography - A security scheme in which a different key is used for encryption and decryption. Key-1 is the public key (i.e., everyone knows it). Key-2 is private, so that only the recipient knows it. In this scheme, it is computationally impossible to derive Key-2 from Key-1.

QuickTime - The industry standard multimedia architecture used by software tool vendors and content creators to store, edit, and play synchronized graphics, sound, video, text, and music. QuickTime was developed originally for the Macintosh, but now used predominately for Internet multimedia.

RDBMS - Relational Database Management System. An application to manipulate data structured in inter-related, dynamically created tables (e.g., Informix, DB2, Oracle, Ingres)

Relaxed Computing - A process that includes both manual and automatic sub processes, or steps. This may include manual steps such as managerial or credit approval mixed into a sequence of events managed by a workflow engine.

RISC - Reduced Instruction Set Computing. Newer processor architecture, with smaller, faster instruction sets.

Router - In data communications, a functional unit used to connect two or more networks. It operates at the network layer (layer 3) of ISO's Open Systems Interconnection-Reference Model. The router reads the network layer address of all packets transmitted and forwards only those addressed to another network.

RPC - Remote Procedure Call. A function that is run on a remote process, typically on a different machine.

RS/6000 - RISC System 6000. An IBM UNIX machine.

RSA - Rivest-Shamir-Adleman (The developers): Works in concert with fast bulk encryption services, such as DES. It manages the exchange of secure keys without prior communications or digital signatures. RSA is a public key system best used for smaller messages and encryption system augmentation.

The Second Industrial Revolution

S/390 - An IBM mainframe.

SAP - Software package produced by SAP AG. This software application includes modules for business processes integrated into a single superstructure for effective use of information. These modules include Sales and Distribution, Manufacturing, Financials, and Human Resources. It is a three-tiered, client/server application.

SCO-UNIX - Santa Cruz Operation. A UNIX implementation on the PC.

Search Engine - Internet application that helps the user find Internet documents and sites with specific information. The search engine has two main facilities; registering and searching. New sites are registered, indexed, and catalogued into the engine's database. When a user asks for documents with certain words or phrases, the engine queries the database for all appropriate pages and responds accordingly.

Server - Software that grants a request. Hardware that runs server software.

SHTTP - Secure Hypertext Transfer Protocol. Terisa Systems' implementation of secure information transmission through the Internet.

SLIP - Serial Line Internet Protocol. A standard for using a regular telephone line (a serial line) and a modem to connect a computer as a real Internet site. SLIP is gradually being replaced by PPP.

SmartCards - They are identification cards used for authentification of a user. Cards such as SecureID and Infokey have been used for remote access verification. HP's SmartCard will be used as a peripheral to the PC for signatures and authentification in Internet electronic commerce and transactions.

SNA - Systems Network Architecture. Software that allows a computer to switch between applications, built on a network protocol and architecture, and hardware architecuture of the same name.

SNMP - Simple Network Mangement Protocol. The TCP/IP standard protocol that is used to manage and control IP gateways and the networks to which they are attached.

SOM - System Object Model. An object-oriented standard defined by IBM for object-to-object and interapplication communication.

SPARC - Sun Microsystems UNIX machine.

SQL - Structured Query Language. This language is an ANSI standard for updating, accessing, and deleting information in relational databases. Informix, Oracle, and other programs support SQL.

SSL - Secure Socket Layer V3.0. A security protocol that provides communications privacy over the Internet. The protocol allows client/server applications to communicate in a way that is designed to prevent eavesdropping, tampering, or message forgery.

SuiteSpot - Netscape's flexible suite of integrated servers that enables business workgroups to communicate and collaborate, utilizing open Internet/Intranet technology. The Netscape SuiteSpot is the intersection of information, applications, and collaboration. These servers include: Catalog Server, Proxy Server, Certificate Authority Server, News Server, MailServer, Enterprise Server, and Directory Server.

SVR4 - System V Release 4. AT&T's definition of UNIX supported by vendors including Unisys, AT&T and SCO.

T-carrier - The generic designator for any of several digitally multiplexed telecommunications carrier systems. T-carrier systems were originally designed to transmit digitized voice signals. Current applications also include digital transmission.

TCP/IP - Transmission Control Protocol/Internet Protocol - This is a standard, connection-oriented, full-duplex, host-to-host protocol used over a packet-switched computer communications network such as the Internet. TCP corresponds closely to the ISO Open Systems Interconnection-Reference Model (OSI-RM) Layer 4 (Transport Layer).

Telephony - The branch of science devoted to the transmission, reception, and reproduction of sounds, such as speech and tones, that represent digits for signaling. Transmission may be via various media, such as wire, optical fibers, or radio.

Telnet - A software service packaged with most operating systems that allows the user to get onto a system over a network as if he or she were using a terminal attached to the system.

Tuxedo - OLTP services for ATLAS.

UDP - Unreliable Datagram Protocol. A low-level network Protocol.

UI - UNIX International. A consortium of vendors developing standards for open systems; sponsored by AT&T, Sun Microsystems, Unisys, and others.

UNIX - An operating system developed by MIT and AT&T that is widely used and supported by virtually all manufacturers. UNIX uses TCP/IP as its standard communications protocol, making UNIX one of the most popular operating system for the Internet.

URL - Uniform Resource Locator. This is the general name for any file transmissible through the web protocols. These file types include FTP, HTTP, and Gopher.

VANs - Value-added networks - Privately owned and maintained computer networks in which network bandwidth is leased for use between geographically disparate sites or between autonomous organizations.

VM - Virtual Machine. An IBM mainframe operating system.

The Second Industrial Revolution

VMS - A proprietary operating system of Digital Equipment Corp.

VSE - An IBM mainframe operating system.

VT100 - Digital's widely-used, character-based terminal.

VTAM - Virtual Telecommunications Access Method. A program that manages remote access to a mainframe.

WAN - Wide Area Network. Any Internet or network that covers an area larger that a single building or campus.

Wavelet - Exploits the temporal redundancies present in an image sequence to reduce an image to a composite of a large set of simpler functions. These waves can be described in a condensed format of only coefficients of known functions.

Weblet - A web application module for use in web pages on the Internet or Intranet.

Web Page - An HTML document on the web, usually one of many that, together, make up a web site

Web Server - Hardware and software devices that can be read on the Internet (or Intranet) through retrieving and displaying documents via hypertext transfer protocol (HTTP). Files can be audio clips, video, graphics, or text.

Webstone - A benchmarking standar for the Internet and web sites, used to test internet servers and web site management software. Similar to SpecInt and SpecFloat, but tor the web specifically.

Windows - A graphical operating system for PCs that runs on top of DOS.

Windows 95 - The newest generation of the graphical operating system for PCs; does not run on top of DOS.

Windows NT - Windows New Technology. A standard operating system developed by Microsoft. Machines with this operating system are used for file servers, application servers, and network/web servers.

WWW - Generally accepted shorthand for the World Wide Web. Also called the web, or W3.

World Wide Web - The mechanism developed by Tim Berners-Lee for CERN physicists to be able to share documents via the Internet. The web allows computer users to access information across systems around the world using URLs (Uniform Resource Locators) to identify files and systems and hypertext links to move between files on the same or different systems.

X86 - Intel's widely-used series of processor chips.

X/OPEN XPG - A set of standards defined by OSF for enhanced code portability.

Yahoo! - One of the more popular Internet search engine sites. This site has its Internet site database categorized for more effective searching.

Additional Reading

Internet:

Angell, David, and Brent Heslop. *The Internet Business Companion.* Reading, MA: Addison-Wesley, 1995.

Comer, Douglas. *The Internet Book: Everything You Need to Know About Computer Networking and How the Internet Works.* Englewood Cliffs, NJ: Prentice-Hall, 1995

Cronin, Mary J. *Doing More Business on the Internet: How the Electronic Highway is Transforming American Companies.* New York: Van Nostrand Reinhold, 1995.

Cronin, Mary J. *Global Advantage on the Internet: From Corporate Connectivity to International Competitiveness.* New York: Van Nostrand Reinhold, 1996

Cronin, Mary J. *The Internet Strategy Handbook.* Boston: Harvard Business School Press, 1996.

Dern, Daniel. *The New User's Guide to the Internet.* New York: McGraw-Hill, 1994.

Drake, William J. *The New Information Infrastructure: Strategies for U.S. Policy.* New York: Twentieth Century Fund Press, 1995.

Ellsworth, Jill. *The Internet Business Book.* New York: Wiley & Sons, 1994.

Additional Readings

Ellsworth, Jill E., and Matthew V. Ellsworth. *The New Internet Business Book.* New York: John Wiley & Sons, Inc., 1996.

Gaffin, Adam. *Everybody's Guide to the Internet.* Cambridge, MA: MIT Press, 1994.

Marine, April ed., *Internet: Getting Started.* Updated Ed. Englewood Cliffs, NJ: Prentice- Hall, 1994.

Meeker, Mary, and Chris De Puy. *The Internet Report.* New York: HarperBusiness, 1996.

Resnick, Rosalind. *The Internet Business Guide.* Indianapolis: SAMS Publishing, 1994.

Smith, Richard J., and Mark Gibbs. *Navigating the Internet.* Indianapolis: SAMS Publishing, 1994.

Strangelove, Michael. *How to Advertise on the Internet: An Introduction to Internet-facilitated Marketing and Advertising.* Ottawa, Canada: Strangelove Internet Enterprises, 1994.

Business:

Barnard, Chester L. *The Functions of the Executive.* Cambridge, MA: Harvard University Press, 1938.

Chandler, Alfred. *The Visible Hand: The Managerial Revolution in American Business.* Cambridge: Harvard University Press, 1977.

Chappell, Tom. *The Soul of a Business: Managing for Profit and the Common Good.* New York: Bantam Books, 1993.

Demming, W.E. *Statistical Adjustment of Data.* 1943

Donovan, John J. *Business Re-engineering with Information Technology.* Englewood Cliffs, NJ: Prentice-Hall, 1994.

Drucker, Peter F. *The Practice of Management.* New York: Harper & Row. 1954.

Hamel, Gary, and C.K. Prahalad. *Competing for the Future (Breakthrough Stratagies for Seizing Control of your Industry and Creating the Markets of Tomorrow).* Boston, MA: Harvard Business School Press, 1994.

Hammer, Michael, and James Champy. *Reengineering the Corporation: A Manifesto for Business Revolution.* New York: HarperBusiness, 1993.

Moore, Geoffrey A. *Crossing the Chasm.* New York: HarperBusiness, 1991.

Peters, Thomas, and R.H Waterman. *In Search of Excellence.* New York: Harper & Row, 1982.

Porter, Michael E. *Competitive Advantage of Their Nation and Their Firm.* New York: The Free Press, 1990.

Porter, Michael E. *Competitive Strategy.* New York: The Free Press, 1985.

Additional Readings

Oster, Sharon M. *Modern Competitive Analysis.* New York: Oxford University Press, 1990.

Reich, Robert B. *The Work of Nations.* New York: Vintage Books, 1991.

Index